We Uyghurs Have No Say

We Uyghurs Have No Say

An Imprisoned Writer Speaks

Ilham Tohti

Translated by Yaxue Cao, Cindy Carter,
and Matthew Robertson

VERSO

London • New York

The editors gratefully acknowledge the assistance of China Change
(https://chinachange.org/) in preparing this book.

First published by Verso 2022
Collection © Verso Books 2022

1 3 5 7 9 10 8 6 4 2

Verso
UK: 6 Meard Street, London W1F 0EG
US: 20 Jay Street, Suite 1010, Brooklyn, NY 11201
versobooks.com

Verso is the imprint of New Left Books

ISBN-13: 978-1-83976-404-2
ISBN-13: 978-1-83976-405-9 (UK EBK)
ISBN-13: 978-1-83976-406-6 (US EBK)

British Library Cataloguing in Publication Data
A catalogue record for this book is available from the British Library

Library of Congress Cataloging-in-Publication Data
A catalog record for this book is available from the Library of Congress

Typeset in Sabon by Biblichor Ltd, Edinburgh
Printed and bound by CPI Group (UK) Ltd, Croydon CR0 4YY

Contents

Preface

Ilham Tohti and the Uyghurs

Rian Thum, University of Manchester

Today Ilham Tohti sits in a Chinese prison, where he is serving a life sentence for the content of his writings. Seven of his students are imprisoned for participating in his intellectual project. Reading through his essays and interviews now, with hindsight, is both illuminating and heartbreaking. Ilham was right, even prescient. He was right that he would be imprisoned, that, in one way or another, "the grim reaper is beckoning." And he was right about the danger that "totalitarian ethnonationalists" in the Chinese Communist Party posed to indigenous groups under their rule, especially Ilham's own people, the Uyghurs.

It turns out that some of Ilham's most dire warnings were understated. From 2017 to 2019, somewhere around 10 percent of the Uyghurs in China, perhaps 1 million people or more, disappeared into what the Chinese government at first called "concentrated transformation education centers" and then renamed "vocational training centers." *The Washington Post* and other sober observers call them concentration camps.[1] In them, Uyghurs have been forced to abandon their language and traditions, renounce their religion, and memorize Party ideology.

---

[1] "New Evidence of China's Concentration Camps Shows Its Hardening Resolve to Wipe out the Uighurs," *The Washington Post*, September 3, 2020.

More recently, many have been transferred to formal prisons or forced labor programs.

Uyghurs outside the prisons and camps experience a different kind of confinement. They are tracked through both elaborate electronic surveillance and old-fashioned totalitarian legwork. Mandatory spyware apps, cameras with facial recognition capabilities, GPS trackers on cars, and predictive policing software bring nearly every movement and utterance under the gaze of the state. To catch what little slips through the electronic net, over 1 million Chinese people of the majority Han ethnic group have been sent to "become family" with Uyghurs, entering rural homes, interviewing their residents, reporting on their habits, and, in many cases, sleeping in their beds. A regional government newspaper, summing up the successes of 2018, boasted of over 10 million overnight "becoming family" stays. In some cases, Han Chinese visitors literally become family, as young men marry Uyghur women in an environment where saying "no" is almost impossible.

The disciplinary measures undergird more direct efforts to destroy the Uyghurs as a group. Children are forcibly separated from their parents and educated in Chinese language and culture. By 2019, roughly half of Xinjiang's middle-school-aged children were placed in compulsory residential schools, with the explicit intent to isolate minority children from the cultural influences of their families. At the same time, an unprecedented program of forced birth control and sterilization has brought the Uyghurs' population growth to nearly zero, all while the state encourages Han parents to have more children.

Ilham, in his prison cell, is almost entirely cut off from the outside world and may not yet be aware of the full scale of the program that has swept up not only his fellow Uyghurs, but also Kazakhs, Kirghiz, and some Hui. The essays collected here, written before Ilham's 2014 arrest, do not address the very latest injustices but instead analyze the economic, political, and discursive structures that were already squeezing Uyghurs when

Ilham began publishing in the 1990s. His work is a reminder that today's internment camps are merely the crescendo of a longer, deeper, and more entrenched dispossession of the Uyghurs. But Ilham's work is not just relevant to the problems of the Uyghurs, or even of minorities in China more generally. It offers a distinctive perspective on global phenomena of marginalization, a perspective honed outside the boundaries of Western-dominated academic conversations like post-colonial studies and the sociology of race. To give one example, his description of minoritized groups as "'social blank space'—an open field in which social experiments can be conducted at will" is at once a fresh response to the Chinese context and immediately recognizable in the global history of colonization and subjugation.

The nuances of Ilham's contributions at both levels— explaining the development of China's current cultural cleansing program and broadening our understanding of marginalization at a global scale—are perhaps best appreciated alongside a basic introduction to their context. This is because, on the one hand, the Uyghurs and other minorities of the People's Republic of China (PRC) are unfamiliar to many readers, and, on the other hand, all of Ilham's writing to date has been undertaken in highly constrained circumstances, in which each word choice was a danger to Ilham and his friends and family. Much was left unsaid and many apparently small gestures have enormous import. For these reasons, I offer here some basic introductory remarks about the Uyghurs and their relationship to China, along with notes on Ilham himself and his relationship to the current Chinese government.

The Uyghurs and China

Ilham is a member of the Uyghur ethnic group, a people whose Turkic language, Central Asian traditions, Islamic heritage, and, in most cases, physical features set them apart from China's largest ethnic group, the Han. The Uyghur homeland has been known by various names over the centuries—Xiyu, Moghulistan, Altishahr, Kashgaria, Little Bukharia, Eastern Turkestan—but today it falls within the borders of China's "Xinjiang" administrative unit. This name, officially bestowed on the region in the late 1800s, gives a hint of how the Uyghurs came under Chinese rule; it is a Chinese word for "new territory."

When China's last imperial dynasty, the Qing, fell to revolutionaries in 1912, intellectuals and politicians trying to build a new Chinese order faced a conundrum. One important source of support for the revolution had been the ethnonationalist idea that the Qing rulers, who were Manchus rather than Chinese, were outsiders—barbarian conquerors prone to misrule. But the Manchus had not only conquered Chinese-inhabited lands. They had also conquered Tibet, Mongolia, and the part of Turkestan they renamed "Xinjiang." What should the Chinese leaders who took control of the Qing state do with this imperial inheritance?

The question was particularly fraught because many Chinese thinkers saw themselves as opponents of imperialism: Manchu, Japanese, and European. Some argued that their new Republic of China should release the other conquered regions. They lost the argument to Sun Yat-sen and others, who redefined "China" to encompass everything the Manchu Qing emperors had controlled, and the "Chinese" as anyone within these borders.

Thus, the Uyghurs today fall under the rule of the People's Republic of China because of the Qing Empire's conquests. This basic fact is widely known among Uyghurs in Xinjiang, spread in part through popular historical fiction. It leads many Uyghurs to dream of an independent state that can recapture what they see as the glory of pre-Qing Eastern Turkestan.

Such aspirations are notably absent from Ilham's writings. Instead, Ilham accepts as a starting point the Uyghurs' membership in the Chinese nation-state, and his criticisms and recommendations employ the current Chinese government's understanding of what China was and is. He is trying to convince a Chinese audience to treat Uyghurs justly, and he unfolds his argument within the premises of official PRC history.

To deal with the great diversity of ethnic identities that the new China encompassed, the Communist Party of China (CCP) borrowed Stalin's theories of ethnicity and nationality, but they made important changes. Whereas Stalin had saved the term "minority" for groups that were dispersed among larger populations (his model case was the Jews), the Communist Party of China labeled all nationalities under its control "minorities"— except, of course the Han. Within their historical homeland (strictly the southern half of Xinjiang), the Uyghurs are actually a numerical majority—what Stalin would have called simply a "nationality." But when considered as part of the larger Chinese nation-state, they are vastly outnumbered by the Han, a power dynamic enshrined in official CCP ideology with the phrase "minority nationality."

Although the Communist Party of China made changes to Stalin's terminology, it kept an important concept, which would serve as the root of Ilham's critique: the idea that all nationalities, whether minorities or not, had certain rights, including political autonomy and the protection of their languages and cultures. When the CCP took power, political autonomy turned out to be a false promise. After their reconquest of Tibet, Xinjiang, and Inner Mongolia, they designated these areas as "Autonomous Regions," but reserved all of the highest political positions for Han Chinese, tightly controlling their policies from Beijing.

Nonetheless, the *theory* of political rights for nationalities survived, and it was formalized in various constitutions and laws (often unenforced) over the course of the PRC's history. This was the ground upon which Ilham fought. His strongest and most frequent request has been for the enforcement of the existing laws on autonomy. He was offering the Communist Party, of which he is a member, a way to extend equality to the Uyghurs without compromising its official ideology or its grip on power.

It is difficult to overstate the sensitivity of these issues within China. CCP laws and pronouncements describe a "nation-state of many nationalities" in which all nationalities are equal. CCP *policy*, by contrast, suggests a lack of confidence in these ideals, and the on-the-ground reality bears undeniable hallmarks of a colonial project. The demography of Xinjiang is a powerful example. In 1946, before the Communist Party took control, Xinjiang had a Han population of 6 percent. By 1982, after decades of CCP policies encouraging and sometimes forcing Han migration to the region, the Han population in Xinjiang stood at 40 percent. The influx of Han settlers has continued in large numbers since, though the proportion of Han Chinese had, until recently, remained steady due to higher Uyghur birth rates. The new, state-induced crash in Uyghur birth rates may well disrupt that balance.

In the PRC's official historical narrative, China has been a victim, but never a perpetrator, of colonialism. What is more, the organization that saved China from the imperialists was purportedly none other than the Communist Party of China. Arguably, Ilham's frequent complaints about the negative effects of Han migration and unequal access to resources had the dangerous effect of pointing up the gap between the Party's actions and its anti-imperialist rhetoric.

In the 1990s, when Ilham began writing about contemporary politics, the Uyghurs as a group were disproportionately impoverished, unemployed, and disempowered. They suffered under more extreme applications of censorship than people in coastal Han-majority cities. And they endured open, unapologetic discrimination in inter-ethnic contexts. While the 1980s had seen a progressive expansion of freedoms for Uyghurs, after 1990 the Chinese state continuously ratcheted up controls on Uyghur communities. By 2008, Uyghurs had suffered passport confiscations, closings of religious sites, and "strike hard" campaigns that targeted individuals with purportedly pro-independence leanings.

Ilham's 2006 call for "long-term resistance against ethno-nationalist totalitarianism" was likely a response to debates within the CCP intellectual establishment about ethnic difference. Some Han scholars had begun calling for an abandonment of existing ethnic ideology, with its rhetoric of autonomy and the protection of distinct cultures, advocating instead a turn toward assimilationist approaches. Even the notional respect for the rights of "minorities" came under attack.

Before long, events conspired to empower the assimilationists. In 2009, a Uyghur protest in the regional capital of Urumqi devolved into ethnic rioting, leaving hundreds dead. In the wake of this tragedy, amid calls from Han residents for stricter treatment of the Uyghurs, assimilationists gained increasing prominence. By 2014, the assimilationist inclination was reflected in local policies, like cash payments for inter-ethnic marriages.

The changes coincided with the rise of China's new leader, Xi Jinping. Xi ushered in two kinds of change that transformed the assimilationist push into the totalitarian ethnonationalist system Uyghurs endure today. The first was a sharp increase in coercive and extralegal measures to eliminate criticism of the Communist Party throughout China. Ilham is only one of its many casualties. The second was a surge in ethnonationalist justifications for CCP rule. The CCP presents itself as the savior of the nation as it always has, but now, more than at any point in the history of the People's Republic, it portrays that nation as essentially Han.

The result is a demonization of everyday Uyghur culture as "backward" and subversive, a resultant desire to transform the Uyghurs into people who act like the Han, and a willingness to use coercive and extralegal measures on a grand scale to achieve this goal. Chinese government documents reveal an enormous network of internment camps, some of them the size of small towns. Firsthand accounts of the camps describe a range of coerced activities, including the chanting of slogans, marching in place, Chinese-language study, memorization of Party ideology, "self-criticisms," denunciation of fellow inmates, and renunciation of Islam, all conducted under military-style discipline, with numerous reports of poor nutrition, enforced silence outside of study sessions, beatings, and endemic torture. Toward the end of 2018 it emerged that many internees were being transferred to forced labor facilities. In the town of Kashgar alone, eighteen new orphanages have been opened, presumably to accommodate the children left behind by parents taken into the camps.

The mass internment system serves as a disciplinary backstop for the state's assimilationist micro-management of Uyghur society outside of the camp walls. Those who are sent to the camps are not charged with any crime, face no trial, and have no means of appeal. Disappearances are swift and arbitrary, empowering security forces to decide the fates of their neighbors without threat of accountability. Children have become a danger to their parents, since their schools encourage them to inform on their parents' religious habits and even the books they own. All of this has created paralyzing fear and desperate compliance among the Uyghur population. Where once there was a thriving trade in banned books (most of them quite innocuous) Uyghurs now proactively destroy their own books in secret. People ask their online contacts to speak in Chinese, not Uyghur, so as to appear patriotic. Some write fervent essays extolling government policies. One Uyghur man officially changed his name to a Chinese name. Meanwhile, coercive birth-control measures aim, in the words of one Chinese scholar-official, to "end the numerical dominance of the Uyghur ethnic group" in Southern Xinjiang, the Uyghur homeland.[2] Many of the Uyghurs' most important historic and religious sites have been wiped off of the landscape. This is the totalitarian ethnonationalist dystopia that Ilham's warnings could have prevented.

---

2 "41st International Law Lecture: The Key to the Stability and Long-Term Security of Xinjiang," *China University of Political Science and Law Research Net* (blog), n.d., sil.cupl.edu.cn.

Ilham Tohti, His Writings, and the Communist Party of China

On September 24, 2014, China's state newspaper devoted an unsigned opinion piece to arguing that Ilham Tohti is *not* "the Chinese Mandela." Rather, the essay falsely claimed, "Ilham Tohti preaches hatred and killing."[3] Many readers of the present volume, when faced with Ilham's actual writings, will be surprised that his open-hearted, deferential pleas for dialogue and reconciliation could inspire such accusations and ultimately land their author in prison. In particular, Ilham called for the full implementation of China's constitution and existing laws on ethnic minorities. As Ilham well knew, this was nonetheless a very dangerous thing to ask of the ruling Communist Party of China, and Ilham's works occasionally refer to the looming threat of imprisonment, which he felt growing with the passing years.

Much of what Ilham wrote is no longer publicly available. He wrote often and addressed multiple audiences, especially on his website, uighur.biz. With the authorities' deletion of his site, some kinds of work have survived better than others. In particular, his Chinese-language essays have circulated among intellectuals and dissidents in China and abroad, leading to their preservation and to their translation in this volume. His interviews with foreign media outlets, notably Radio Free Asia, have of course survived as well. In 2020, the Ilham Tohti Institute in Germany announced that it had recovered over three thousand articles from Ilham's former website. Many of these are now available in Chinese at uyghurbiz.org.

What Ilham wrote in Uyghur is more difficult to find. As I write I am unable to access any of these essays, and therefore unable to check any new claims I might be tempted to make about them. But this is how I described Ilham after consulting

---

3 See "China Voice: Mandela Analogy Shows Ignorance of History," *People's Daily* Online, September 24, 2014, en.people.cn.

what could still be found online in 2010: "Tohti stands out for his commitment to working within the established Chinese political order . . . He is an outspoken and articulate critic of many discriminatory Chinese policies, but his writings do not challenge the ideological foundations of the People's Republic or the legitimacy of Chinese rule in Xinjiang."[4]

Ilham's life story, and his writing, are the tale of what could have been, the perpetually and repeatedly missed opportunities for "integration," reconciliation, and accommodation. In each prescient essay, we see the choices that Chinese authorities turned down, roads toward justice they refused to take. Ilham offers up narratives of a generous party and a just Chinese nation-state, narratives free for the authorities' taking, narratives that could permit them to gracefully compromise without ceding power. These narratives were not only rejected but used as evidence for the judicial but ultimately illegal imprisonment of their author.

Calling Ilham a "Chinese Mandela" captures his magnanimity, his patience, his moral gravity, and his unfathomable courage in the face of brutal imprisonment, but it is important to remember that Ilham is not a politician and does not consider himself an activist. He sees himself as a scholar, and his contributions in that register deserve serious attention. Ilham is the preeminent Uyghur thinker on the status of indigenous peoples within the world's largest state, the People's Republic of China. His essays offer insights into a world of multipolar colonialism. The West's monopoly on imperialism has been broken, if in fact it ever existed. And Western thinkers' satisfaction with their own conceptual frameworks of difference—race, ethnicity, indigeneity—must eventually give way to curiosity about the very different ideas that underlie China's enthusiastic embrace of its imperial inheritance.

---

4 Alexa Olsen, "Angry Minority Finds a Voice on Chinese Campus," nwasianweekly.com, January 7, 2010.

The situation of the Uyghurs is more dire than it has ever been, and the prospects for Ilham's early release are more meager. But given Ilham's prescience in so many matters, we can perhaps take some hope from his own optimism. On the very day he received his life sentence, September 24, 2014, Ilham prepared a statement in response, which included these words: "I am convinced that China will become better, and that the constitutional rights of the Uyghur people will, one day, be honored."

Articles

The Source of Xinjiang Ethnic Tensions as I See Them

Written in 2005, this essay was first posted on Uyghur Online in May, 2007. Ilham Tohti founded Uyghur Online, a Chinese-language website, in 2006 to bridge the information gap between the Han population and the Uyghur people and to facilitate understanding of Xinjiang and the Uyghurs. The site published original writing as well as content from other news sources on events in Xinjiang and human rights in general. Over time it attracted a readership in the millions and hosted sometimes heated discussions. Ilham moderated some of the forums to block hate speech and separatist sentiment. Despite this, Uyghur Online was repeatedly shut down by the Chinese government; its server, when eventually moved overseas, suffered cyberattacks. It permanently went offline after Ilham's arrest in January 2014.

Urumqi is the capital of the Xinjiang Uyghur Autonomous Region. From the outside, the capital of this ethnic minority autonomous region doesn't differ much from any other city in northern China—but in fact, the issues surrounding the native people of Xinjiang are the most sensitive of all five of China's autonomous regions.

The Uyghur Autonomous Region was established in Xinjiang in 1955, and Uyghurs were full of hope and expectation of being able to administer their own land. As time passed, however, they began to sense that the so-called right to autonomous rule existed in name only. This impression extended to outsiders who came to Urumqi and other cities and walked the streets—they certainly didn't feel that the place had the air of being under local governance. A main reason for this was that in Urumqi, a city of around 2 million, three quarters are Han. Actual Uyghurs can only be found around the Southern Gate of the city near the Erdao Bridge market. Elsewhere in Xinjiang's cities, factories, enterprises, banks, customs, airports, government offices, oilfields . . . it's the same. It goes without saying that this is even more true when it comes to the enormous paramilitary brigade, the Xinjiang Production and Construction Corps, which has absolutely nothing to do with locals.

The peoples of Xinjiang, Kazakhstan, Kyrgyzstan, Tajik-istan, and other neighboring countries in Central Asia are similar to Uyghurs culturally, linguistically, and in appearance—there are even many related families spanning the countries, and they used to cross borders at will. Given this circumstance, the Chinese government instituted an "open toward the West" policy, using trade and commerce to dissipate any potential ethnic conflicts between Xinjiang and Central Asian countries. Hundreds of thousands of visitors enter Xinjiang annually, the majority of them from Russia and Central Asia, coming to do business or see family.

Apart from this, China has adopted an internal/external dual-track approach for defusing ethnic problems. At the foreign policy level, China formed the Shanghai Cooperation Organization with Russia, Kazakhstan, Tajikistan, Kyrgyzstan, and Uzbekistan, which meets every year in late August. One of the important issues they address is the ethnic question. Domestically, as an important aspect of resolving ethnic problems, the government has fast-tracked economic development in Xinjiang, whose land mass is one-sixth of China's territory. And yet, this beautiful and fertile land has come more and more to resemble simply a playground for immigrants from the interior.

Local peoples in Xinjiang have reaped very few of the benefits of economic development. Instead, they're left with unemploy-ment, poverty, barren land, and a continued influx of immigrants from elsewhere in China. The local population increasingly feels that it's being marginalized. In the development of natural resources in ethnic areas, the state has not really thought about how local people are supposed to benefit; nor have they paid much attention to driving local economic development, in particular agricultural development; nor have they sought to transition local people from the countryside to new industries in urban centers for work. This pattern has led to a chain of social outcomes that have brought about a hidden crisis. The differential in power has made it difficult for Uyghurs to find work, and experts believe that may lead to greater incidents of crime, and a tendency to violence and support for splittism and ethnic opposition to the state.

The adversity Uyghurs face can be seen clearly in their high rates of unemployment and poverty. This data shows that Xinjiang is the only place in the world where local university graduates have a lower status than migrant farmers. Official media have reported that of the roughly 1 million Han migrant workers who come to Xinjiang for casual labor every year, between 10 and 15 percent of them plan to settle down there. At the same time, around 1 million Uyghur farm laborers are made "redundant," hundreds of thousands of Uyghurs are forced to leave their homeland to seek casual work in the interior, and tens of thousands of Uyghur children become vagrants. [Han] migrant workers from the interior are able to come to Xinjiang to seek work and improve their living conditions, but for Uyghurs—even though they're willing to sacrifice more, working long hours for low pay—their opportunities for finding work locally are minimal.

These days the situation of Uyghurs is not too bad, especially Uyghurs from southern Xinjiang; a few of them even become students at top universities. However, Uyghurs overall are underemployed, or make a living in informal or marginal industries where they have to eke out a living on low pay. For the government departments that spread propaganda about "ethnic solidarity," these Uyghurs are heroes—yet they don't enjoy the rights they're entitled to in the Chinese constitution, nor dignity.

Resolving the question of ethnic inequality requires more than merely focusing on poverty-stricken regions. Policy design needs to focus on minority ethnicity households in poorer regions and guarantee that they not be subjected to discrimination (for instance, in the labor market), thus expanding their opportunities and removing their social isolation and exclusion. Policy should also explicitly acknowledge that there are some practices (including compensatory behaviors) that, while satisfying to minorities' short-term needs, will simply exacerbate inequality in the long run.

The majority of Uyghurs and other minorities in Xinjiang live in remote, rural areas, and their living standards are typically below that of the Han population. To what extent is this situation caused primarily by *differences* between economic features, such as the level of educational attainment and access to land, and not the low rate of return on those factors? Among minority ethnic groups, is there a culture that constantly reinforces conditions of poverty, and which then serves to confirm the prejudices against them and thus discrimination? One of the reasons for the lower standard of living of minorities is that the areas they live in have a low level of productivity. These regions share the following characteristics: rugged terrain, poor infrastructure, few opportunities for interfacing with the nonagricultural labor market, and relatively poor educational opportunities. Low mobility contributes to the stickiness in differentials between living standards in different regions. And yet this author has found that there are sometimes significant differences within individual regions, even after household idiosyncrasies are taken into account. Thus, scholars have found that the most important reason for inequality between ethnic groups is the rate of return on productivity factors.

However, it is not that minority ethnicities get a low rate of return on their productivity across the board. There is evidence of compensatory behaviors—for instance, their rate of return on geographical location (even if it's remote or unsuited to residences) is relatively high, even though this is insufficient to compensate for their massive consumption differential with other ethnic groups.

The key is to eliminate discrimination against minorities in the labor market and elsewhere, so as to expand their options and at the same time change the conditions that keep them isolated and excluded.

Employment is a major bottleneck, and educational resources in Xinjiang need to be far more tilted toward helping minority students. Forcing children with completely different mother tongues to compete from the same starting line is highly unfair.

As Uyghurs continue to remain underemployed, as urbanization gains pace, and as Han farmers acquire land, the traditional living space for minorities is increasingly constrained by the pace of economic development.

If Han people and government policies don't consider the living space available for minorities, the outlook for Xinjiang is not optimistic. Military force can't resolve these problems. To this day, all emphases on Xinjiang's energy resources have been in terms of the interests of Han people and the rest of China, which makes me truly grieve for Xinjiang!

The rapid development of the petroleum sector in Xinjiang is shown in the constant increase of oil production, storage, and revenues. Added to this is general local economic development, with an increase in migrants from the Chinese interior, environmental pollution, improvement in infrastructure around oil towns, including more roads and entertainment venues, and exports of oil and other goods from Xinjiang to the rest of the country. Along with this, the proportion of the native population to new immigrants is declining, economic reform continues (mainly in mining and exploration and acquisitions of Xinjiang enterprises by companies from the interior), and nominal state income is increasing, but widespread unemployment remains a problem in the nonpetroleum sector and high levels of poverty persist among minorities. Unequal wealth distribution has led to wider discrepancies among Xinjiang residents, making the gap between the rich and poor extremely severe. As a result, vulnerable groups that have been socially excluded are unable to enjoy the same education, healthcare, and employment opportunities as favored population groups.

The core question in Xinjiang is the lack of civil rights of minorities in Xinjiang! The central government should earnestly study and investigate the problems with its ethnic policies in Xinjiang. The government should implement and improve the Law on Regional National Autonomy in good faith, and see to it that local people are treated equally and enjoy the same opportunities to participate in the economic development of the Xinjiang Uyghur Autonomous Region.

The Need to Mount Long-Term Resistance to Totalitarianism and Ethnonationalist Chauvinism

Published in September 2006 on Uyghur Online.

As part of our self-understanding as a people, the most important thing we need to do is carry out long-term resistance to totalitarian ideology and ethnonationalist chauvinism to prevent it from coming back and occupying our national ideology and political sphere.

For an ethnonationalist girded by totalitarianism, minority peoples are in essence a "social blank space"—an open field in which social experiments can be conducted at will. This picture of a supposed "blank space" gives rise to all manner of fanciful, imagined possibilities. The millennia-long historical culture of Uyghurs, Mongols, Hui, and other ethnic groups, as well as their contributions to the nation and their real existence as distinct peoples, count as nothing in the eyes of ethnonationalist-chauvinist totalitarians—they can be disregarded and ignored entirely. Yet for the peoples themselves, these are sacred things. For these and many, many other reasons, the needs of minority peoples and the demands of ethnonationalist totalitarians are in irreconcilable conflict.

By using slogans like "developing terra nullius" and "developing the wasteland" and other ignorant slogans [about the colonization of Xinjiang by Han people], countless young people have been influenced to treat minority ethnic people and regions with utter disregard. These slogans inculcate them with the idea that they're the pioneers on this land. Fortunately, historical facts will restore everything, and it has become a part of the spiritual world of all

9

living in Xinjiang to learn about the great, inspiring, and exciting culture of this land, including its social economy and ethnic history. But we must always remember the lessons history has given us about ethnonationalist totalitarianism, and this will always remain a painful memory in the history of our people.

If ethnonationalist totalitarianism really gains the upper hand, the only outcome will be to lead this great nation and people to a dead end. The great misfortune is that the state today promotes the "construction of a harmonious society," and "harmonious China"—for example, with websites like Han Net (www.cnhan.com), which use the most advanced and expedient internet technologies—they're firmly pushing for, propagandizing, and insisting on ethnonationalism. This is not an accident—and seeing this fact as an accident of history is an unforgivable mistake. Looking at this phenomenon with merely superficial contempt, and as a perfectly understandable historical ethnic experience, will serve to obscure the true dangers that lurk in the future. We all know how history punishes its lazy students.

Of course, in our country's governmental and legal system, ethnonationalist totalitarianism has no place. Though we can indeed use a few isolated phenomena to explain these circumstances, the key is that we also step back and look at the big picture. There is an irreconcilable conflict between the closed nature of ethnonationalist chauvinism and the preconditions for technological innovation, which include the free flow of information. As time passes, the attempt to maintain such control will be increasingly inefficient, and will in the end lead down a blind alley. Ethnonationalism in the context of an open internet and technological sector is bound to lose out. And a people caught in an ethnonationalist totalitarian ideology will find themselves falling behind and will ultimately fail.

The most important thing for our national consciousness is to wage long-term resistance against ethnonationalist totalitarianism and prevent it from once again invading and occupying our social consciousness and political system.

Isn't It Time to Rethink China's Ethnic Policies?

This essay, posted on Uyghur Online on November 12, 2009, is an abbreviated version of a speech Ilham Tohti gave on November 6, at Minzu University of China, under the watch of domestic security police.

Ilham Tohti here refers to several well-known violent incidents. Beginning on March 10, 2008, a series of protests had erupted in Lhasa, the capital city of the Tibetan Autonomous Region, to mark the anniversary of the failed 1959 Tibetan uprising against Chinese rule. On March 14, hundreds of monks and nuns from various temples were met with force by Chinese police and military units, and the protests spread to include many other Tibetans as well as, eventually, people across the world. Clashes occurred across the Tibetan plateau, and police cars, shops, and government buildings were burned. The Central Tibetan Administration reported thousands of arrests. The Chinese government framed the protests as a secessionist movement supported by "hostile foreign forces."

The next year, on June 25 and 26, 2009, violence broke out between Han Chinese and Uyghur workers in a large toy factory in Shaoguan, Guangdong province, over accusations that Uyghur male workers had sexually assaulted Han female workers. Two Uyghur workers died and hundreds were injured. This ethnic brawl sparked protests on July 5, 2009, in Urumqi, the capital city of the Xinjiang Uyghur Autonomous Region, where Uyghurs called for an investigation into the Shaoguan incident. These protests began peacefully but turned into violent clashes themselves, and eventually hundreds were detained, imprisoned, or disappeared.

Four months after the events in Urumqi, many people inside and outside China are focused on what Beijing is going to do about its ethnic minorities problem. Last year there was the "March 14 Incident" in Lhasa, and now we've recently had the "July 5th Incident" in Urumqi as well as the earlier "June 26 Incident" in Shaoguan. Both the Chinese and foreign media are constantly asking: "Is something wrong with China's policies toward ethnic minorities?"

Politburo member and Guangdong Party secretary Wang Yang told a foreign reporter in Guangzhou on July 29 that it's time to reconsider China's policies toward ethnic minorities, but he didn't say anything specific about what mistakes had been made or put forward any plan for resolving them. He said, "The policies themselves definitely need to be revised based on the actual situation. China is a multiethnic country, and there will be problems if we don't make some adjustments right away."

For Wang Yang, who is close to President Hu Jintao, to say this kind of thing shows that the Chinese leadership is carefully considering how to deal with the Xinjiang problem and revise the country's sensitive policies toward ethnic minorities. Earlier, however, vice-chairman of the State Ethnic Affairs Commission (SEAC) Wu Shimin said at a press conference in Beijing: "China's ethnic minorities policies have been successful at promoting unity, equality and harmony between all ethnicities."

In a detailed report on Wu Shimin's comments on China's ethnic minorities policies, the Beijing correspondent for the Swiss newspaper *Neue Zürcher Zeitung* wrote: "Scientific investigation and people's personal experience repeatedly show, however, that when it comes to core issues like people's well-being, healthcare, and religious freedom, the realities for most Uyghurs and Tibetans are not the same."

In Xinjiang, the average life expectancy, infant mortality rate, rate of urbanization, per capita income, employment rate, and other important indicators are all worse for Uyghurs than for Han. In reality, Uyghurs' autonomy and religious freedom are quite limited. For example, even though the top officials in many levels of government in autonomous regions are ethnic minorities, the real power and actual oversight of policy implementation in those regions is tightly controlled by the party secretaries, all of whom are Han. In Xinjiang, students in schools at all levels and of all types aren't permitted to enter mosques and religious education is banned.

Wu Shimin says, "The economic crisis intensified unemployment in Xinjiang" and "Xinjiang isn't one of China's developed areas." But he's not willing to face the problem. (In fact, the high unemployment rate among Uyghurs is not something that has come about only in the past few years.)

Since the "March 14th," "June 26th," and "July 5th" incidents, the authorities still keep pinning the blame on overseas Tibetan and Xinjiang independence forces. As usual, the Xinjiang authorities attribute the causes, action, and responsibility for the incident on the "Three Forces" (of separatism, terrorism, and religious extremism). But who instigated the incident in Shaoguan? Do you mean to say that the government acted flawlessly, without any mistakes? Were there really no internal factors or societal causes? Once again, people are left without the facts. We need to rethink our ethnic policies.

It's Time to Rethink China's Ethnic Policies

Globalization makes it more and more possible for major events that happen in one country to be connected to external factors. But this doesn't mean that the Chinese government can be indifferent to domestic ethnic problems. In fact, no matter how important external factors may be, the main factors are still internal. Actually, the ethnic conflicts in Xinjiang and Tibet and the series of mass social disturbances in places like Weng'an and Shishou have exposed serious crises hidden in Chinese society.

These ethnic conflicts show that we must put building ethnic harmony on the agenda. Looking long term, if we don't face the problems and just cover them up, more ethnic conflict could erupt at any time. Major bloody incidents are occurring during China's "flourishing age" of "stability above all else." Doesn't this series of ethnic conflicts mean that we need to rethink China's ethnic policies? I would answer yes: it's time for China's ethnic policies to be revised.

Uyghur–Han resentment is getting worse and has been building for quite some time. The Han are increasingly unhappy because they think government policies give ethnic minorities like the Uyghurs preferential treatment. Meanwhile, we Uyghurs think that the Han in Xinjiang have become a very special group that the government treats better and that Uyghurs have been marginalized in all areas. Now the problem has been exposed, and we must rethink domestic ethnic policies. If we want to achieve ethnic harmony, we must start by rethinking the ethnic policies adopted since the founding of the PRC.

In fact, ethnic problems pose a dilemma in any country. During the thirty years of "reform and opening," the Xinjiang Uyghur Autonomous Region (XUAR) experienced an upsurge of economic construction and made great progress. However, like other regions of China, development has been uneven and there has been more focus on construction than protection. The gap between rich and poor continues to grow and social conflicts have accumulated. If you have officials in some places who govern in simplistic, crude, and corrupt ways, these conflicts will inevitably intensify.

However, it's too one-sided and simplistic to attribute all of these common problems to ethnic conflict. Since political reform has stalled, there's no effective oversight or limits on power. Even though there has been rapid economic development in the rest of China, corruption is serious, and unjust distribution has led to a serious gap between rich and poor.

I believe that the XUAR is also experiencing the same problems as the rest of China, such as the problem of how to deal with the unfair distribution of wealth, the problem of environmental and resource protection, and how to protect and promote ethnic culture. But this can't be a reason for covering up the real ethnic problems that exist or, even worse, an excuse for those in power to evade responsibility and cover up the problems of policies and of the political system. The top priority for the government is to rethink its ethnic policies.

Ethnic Autonomy Is Facing an Even Bigger Challenge

A string of different incidents in ethnic regions have given people living in the rest of China their first glimpse of how ethnic relations, which have been far from the center of the political agenda for many years, aren't as harmonious as they had thought they were. At the same time economic centers were being established in ethnic regions, estrangement and hidden problems were also accumulating. For a majority of the ethnic population, the emergence and suppression of these incidents will enter the historical memory of a generation. Meanwhile, the Chinese public is beginning to question the policies of ethnic autonomy, and there is a lot of criticism of ethnic policies. There are even some radicals who call for the authorities to scrap the current policies. Haven't we reached the point where China's ethnic policies urgently need to be revised?

Actually, in recent years there have been fierce debates within the academic community about current ethnic policies. To resolve ethnic problems inside a multiethnic country, is it better to rely on a "political transformation" approach of institutional arrangements or a "cultural transformation" approach of seeking resolution between different groups?

In 2004, Ma Rong published an academic article in the *Journal of Peking University* entitled "A New Path to Understanding Ethnic Relations: 'Depoliticizing' Ethnic Problems." In it, he recommended abandoning ethnic policies inherited from the

Soviet Union that aimed at the "political transformation" of ethnic minority groups and instead learning from the successful American model of "culturally transforming" ethnic groups in order to build a national ethnic framework of "political unity" and "cultural diversity."

For the past few months, quite a few people both inside and outside China have been discussing whether there's a need to reform the system of ethnic autonomy. The vast majority advocate doing away with ethnic autonomy, which is a bad idea. I've found that so far these discussions have been quite one-sided, their vision limited, and their thinking quite narrow and old-fashioned.

I worry that if policy research and planning follows down this road it will be counterproductive and make things even worse. Even though there are strong doubts being voiced about ethnic policies, the Fourth Plenum called for remaining firm in terms of the theory of ethnic affairs and ethnic regional autonomy. In other words, the government's response is that it will not make any changes right now.

Last month, during the governing party's commemoration of the sixtieth anniversary of the founding of the PRC, the government continued in its old practices of promoting ethnic unity in what can be called a large-scale, high-density manner. Exhibitions were held celebrating the achievements in constructing Xinjiang and Inner Mongolia and a set of "Ethnic Unity Columns" erected on Tiananmen Square. The State Ethnic Affairs Commission (SEAC) responded to press questions on ethnic policies, and the State Council Information Office (SCIO) published a white paper entitled *Ethnic Policy and Common Prosperity and Development of All Ethnic Groups*. They also held a large-scale "National Ethnic Unity Awards Ceremony," at which Hu Jintao delivered a speech on ethnic unity.

All of this shows that ethnic problems are once again a central issue in China's political life. SEAC Director Yang Jing said that ethnic unity was like air: when it's good, you don't notice it, but as soon as there's a problem everyone comes to realize how valuable it is. Since ethnic policy is currently facing a major crisis, ethnic problems have once again become a central focus of the leadership.

Throughout the exhibition of achievements, the press event by the officials from the SEAC, and the SCIO white paper, however, one finds only false presentations of peace and prosperity when it comes to the issue of ethnic unity. They make it appear as if all ethnic groups live together in harmony, all thriving amid growth and prosperity. There's a false sense that people from all the nation's ethnic groups are filled with confidence on ethnic matters. Yes, "revolutionary romanticism" has given us images of "Long Live the Unity of All Chinese Ethnic Peoples." The relevant ethnic policies are explained as they have long been articulated, with no new significance.

After seeing all of this, a question naturally comes to mind: If the direction of ethnic policy is correct, the measures being taken are effective, and there is coordinated development of society, economy, and culture in ethnic regions, then why would there be such serious problems?

I therefore believe that, while positive propaganda on ethnic issues is absolutely necessary, we also need to undertake serious and deep rethinking. If we don't carry out this sort of deep reflection and fix the problems with our ethnic policies in a systematic and thorough manner, China's ethnic problems will get worse and worse—perhaps even worse than we could possibly imagine. The current way of doing things and understanding is limited to purely technical measures. We still haven't tried to understand and reflect on ethnic work with a stronger emphasis on politics, law, and humanistic care.

There are some problems that have to be considered in context. We should seek causes at a much deeper level if we hope to apply the right cure for the ailment and ensure that our ethnic policies are in tune with reality. Whether you blame an incident on ethnic conflict, separatism, ethnic religious policies, or terrorist activity, at root it is caused by the existence of "problems." The officials say that the

Xinjiang problem is not an ethnic problem, a problem of policy, a religious or human rights problem, and certainly not a problem of inequality. But if not these, then what sort of a problem is it?

I prefer to look for the origins in history and examine the entire sequence of events leading up to this ethnic problem.

Uyghur and Tibetan Autonomy Didn't Begin with the CCP

The first thing we need to be clear about is that Uyghur and Tibetan autonomy didn't begin when the CCP took power. Over the long span of history, Xinjiang and Tibet were independent, semi-independent, or highly autonomous for the vast majority of the time. This is a historical fact! As long as you respected the people there and respected their right to autonomy, there was stability in Xinjiang and Tibet. If not, there were uprisings, riots, wars, and separatism.

If you were a Uyghur faced with a powerful Han people, what would you do? There are 1.3 billion Han, but only 10 million Uyghurs. All ethnic groups want to protect their own culture and ethnic characteristics, rather than assimilate. Uyghurs are no exception.

When people say that Uyghurs are the least Chinese members of the Chinese nation, they're probably talking about our distinctive culture, language, religion, race, and so on. Xinjiang's economy has grown at a fast pace, but Uyghurs continue to have high rates of poverty and unemployment. The Han have an old saying: "Judge another's feelings by one's own." It means that you have to put yourself in someone else's shoes and consider problems from their perspective. If we could only do more of that, wouldn't there be many fewer conflicts and tragedies in the world?

The reason that there have been continuous ethnic conflicts between Uyghurs and Han is because Uyghurs have always believed in preserving and developing their own culture, religious beliefs, and language. People want to live in dignity, which means they need an equal environment in which to live and develop. A people should be respected and not be marginalized and made to feel like strangers in their own homeland.

From the mid-eighteenth century to the beginning of the twentieth century, there were dozens of uprisings in Xinjiang, both large and small. There was the Revolt of the Altishahr Khojas (1758), the Mailamu Incident (1760), the Ush Uprising (1765), violence against Qing military camps (1767), the Zia-ud-din Incident (1815), the Jahangir Khoja Revolt (1820–28), the Khoqand Invasion (1830), the Huwan Incident (1845), the Shah Mu'min Incident (1845), the Revolt of the Seven Khojas (1847), the Divan Quli Invasion (1852), the Husayn Ishan Khoja Invasion (1855), the Tarbagatai Incident (1855), the Kucha Uprising (1857), the Wali Khan Invasion (1857), the Epaer Incident (1860), the Yang Sanxing Uprising (1863), the Xinjiang peasant rebellion of 1864, the Russian invasion (1871–82), the Yaqub Beg Invasion (1865–77), the Wu Lezi Incident (1899), Tuer Bake Incident (1907), and the Hami uprisings of 1907 and 1911–14.

Although the causes of all these various revolts and uprisings were different, some of them involving intervention by external forces, their most basic reason was that the Uyghurs of this area, whose culture was vastly different from the one that arose in the Central Plains, wanted respect, wanted their cultural rights, and opposed oppression.

After Xinjiang governor Yang Zengxin was assassinated in 1928, his successor Jin Shuren oppressed and exploited the people. The worst was his oppression of Muslims through a levy on butchered animals and a ban on the Hajj. In Hami, over the opposition of the local people, he carried out a campaign of land confiscation and redistribution to Han settlers that ultimately sparked a revolt by local Uyghur Muslims. The 1933 Hami Rebellion, which spread throughout Xinjiang, led to the first popular movement toward independence and has been called by scholars the "founding national movement of East Turkestan."

Eleven years later, in August 1944, what has been called the second East Turkestan nationalist movement erupted. In what local people call the "November Revolution," the "East Turkestan Republic" was announced and split from China. This is what the CCP officials later called the "Three Districts Revolution." These tragic historical events have become a part of our people's collective memory.

It's not only that the "Xinjiang Problem" has long existed—it has also continued throughout the past sixty years of Communist rule. Violent unrest has been frequent in the XUAR and has grown larger in scale and geographic scope. During the Cultural Revolution, many areas witnessed a great "cross-border exodus" as the local population fled to the Soviet Union. In other words, the Uyghur resistance has been ongoing now for several generations. If there weren't serious problems in the XUAR, why would this be? Knowing the origins and background for the problems helps us understand where the trouble lies, suggests alternatives for a plan for solving the problem, and gives us insight into ethnic people's psychology and motivation to resist.

Why hasn't rapid economic growth in the XUAR led to support from Uyghurs? Isn't it worth reflecting on why they have instead become increasingly dissatisfied? Isn't it because of the reasons I've just stated? We're at the point where we need to reconsider our ethnic policies, otherwise the negative consequences will be too dreadful to contemplate!

We should recognize the special nature of the XUAR. Uyghurs have their own religious beliefs and unique language and culture. The brilliance of human society is a product of its many religions and cultures. We spare no effort to protect endangered animals, so why not protect this unique human culture? Why don't we preserve Uyghurs' unique language and culture, just as we preserve endangered animals or the world's cultural artifacts?

Xinjiang's economy has grown very rapidly for many years, but this kind of rapid growth has been accompanied by a huge influx of immigrants from the east (the majority of whom were mobilized or organized by the government), and this has had a serious impact on the unique local culture. Since 1949, Uyghurs have gone from making up 79 percent of the population in Xinjiang to around 46 percent, while the percentage of Han rose from 4.8 percent to around 40 percent during the same period. This doesn't count the several million registered members of the "floating" or transient population and officers and enlisted men in the People's Liberation Army and People's Armed Police. Shouldn't we reflect on whether this type of economic growth is something Uyghurs should welcome?

The Crux of the Problem: Uyghurs Ought to Enjoy Legal Autonomy

In my view, the July 5th Incident was not simply a problem of outside forces, an ethnic problem, and especially not a problem of so-called interference by international anti-China forces. That's because these problems existed before, they exist today, and they will exist for a long time to come. So, you can talk about these three issues, but it won't help you solve the real problem. The key is to solve the problem of rights, meaning the right to ethnic regional autonomy and other rights that the Uyghur people have been granted by law.

Perhaps people will ask: Why are more and more people calling China's policies on ethnic regional autonomy into question? It's true that according to the law Xinjiang is a Uyghur autonomous region. At its founding, the CCP promised to grant minorities the right to self-determination. In 1947, the Kuomintang (KMT) government and representatives of the Xinjiang people reached an eleven-point agreement promising a high degree of autonomy. After taking power, the CCP no longer spoke in terms of "ethnic self-determination" and replaced it with a system of "ethnic autonomy," a model that was accepted by Uyghurs. In 1955, the party and government legally established the XUAR based on this political promise. The Chinese

Constitution and Law on Ethnic Regional Autonomy clearly established that ethnic autonomous areas have the right to autonomy. Uyghurs looked forward to the implementation of the right to their own autonomy!

It's therefore not accurate to say simply that China's ethnic problems were inherited from the Soviet model. For example, according to Soviet law ethnic autonomous entities had self-determination, but there is no basis for self-determination under Chinese law. The Soviet Union continued to stick to ethnic policies based on orthodox Marxist-Leninist theory, which easily enabled the Soviet republics to become independent after the dissolution of the Soviet Union. But whatever ethnic policy you adopt, resolving ethnic problems must apply principles of reason, including respect for the law, and avoid an obsession with violence. Relying on high-pressure tactics can solve problems for a time, but not in a fundamental way. You see that the former Soviet Union didn't have this problem, and of course policies of forced assimilation won't deal with ethnic problems either.

Chinese law clearly states that ethnic autonomy is a fundamental state institution. The law also makes clear that Xinjiang is a Uyghur Autonomous Region and that Uyghurs are an autonomous ethnic group. According to the 1982 Constitution and the 1984 Regional Ethnic Autonomy Law, ethnic minorities have the right to use and develop their own spoken and written language. Members of ethnic minorities may hold key positions in local administrative bodies. They have the right to preserve their own folkways and customs and enjoy religious freedom. They have the right to use their ethnic languages to develop schools of all levels and types and the government has the responsibility to establish ethnic schools. According to this law, Uyghur is the working language of governments, courts, procuratorates, and judicial administration bodies at all levels. Autonomous regional governments have the right to review state law and may make accommodations or refuse if a law is not suited to the actual local situation. The Regional Ethnic Autonomy Law says further that business enterprises that exploit resources in ethnic regions should respect the interests of the local people and that you should give hiring preference to local people.

Have these laws and policies really been implemented in Xinjiang? Just think about it: Real power in each of the autonomous regions of course belongs to the party and has almost always been placed in the hands of Han. Early on, there was the Uyghur chairman of the XUAR, Saifuddin Azizi, but since then all of the top power-holders have been Han. Of the nine chairmen of the XUAR, two were Han—Long Shujin (1968–72) and Wang Feng (1978–79).

Conflicts in ethnic regions like the one that occurred on July 5 are essentially institutional problems—the result of irrational institutions. I'm not saying that ethnic problems don't exist. But I want to emphasize the point that the political institutions and system set up since 1949 are largely responsible for the conflicts we see in ethnic regions today. The ideology of the Communist Party is fundamentally proletarian dictatorship, culturally emphasizing atheism and politically structured as a closed system under centralized power. All of this has created many obstacles to ethnic regions being able to realize the kind of ethnic autonomy provided for in the constitution. The ideology of atheism is a serious blow to our culture and religion.

Since "reform and opening," Xinjiang has experienced tremendous economic growth. The government has invested a great deal, but Uyghurs are unhappy that they haven't enjoyed the benefits that have come from the exploitation of the resources of their region. From 2002 to 2008, Xinjiang's economy doubled, but 60 percent of the region's economic output still depends on resource extraction, particularly oil, coal, and natural gas. In 1949, Han made up only 4.8 percent of the population; by 2007 it was about 40 percent. Statistical data reveal the inequality between ethnic groups. Around 90 to 92 percent of Uyghurs live in rural villages, while Xinjiang's urbanization rate is approximately 10 percent above the national rate. Last year, government statistics showed that the annual per capita GDP in Xinjiang was 19,000 yuan, whereas the average income in rural areas was 3,800 yuan (US$560) and the average income in southern Xinjiang's rural areas was even lower than that. For example, according to government data the average annual income of rural people in Hotan Prefecture was only 2,226 yuan, and there are many villages in southern Xinjiang where the average annual income is only around 1,500 yuan. Most of the reclaimable land where the drought level isn't too serious, arable land with favorable conditions and farms with water resources and government investment, is controlled by the Xinjiang Production and Construction Corps, the quasi-military organization made up primarily of Han.

Han control has gone beyond natural resources and large-scale agriculture. For example, when the regional government hires civil servants the vast majority of positions are clearly designated for Han. In state-owned enterprises, it long ago became almost part of the "culture" to hire mainly Han. Han have even begun to take over the production of traditional Uyghur products, from traditional markets to Muslim foods. For example, the right to supply halal food products for flights heading to Xinjiang and Muslim countries has been cornered by Xinjiang Jiayu Industrial & Trading Co., a company that produces forty-six different types of products and is owned by the Han businesswoman Huo Lanlan. According to the *Wall Street Journal*, Huo Lanlan admits that most of her company's 300 employees are Han. The company has a few Uyghur employees, like a woman who works as a cleaner, but most of the positions belong to Han. Of course, she adds that all halal food companies are required to have Uyghur employees. Moreover, even though many of the passengers on flights between Urumqi and Kashgar are Uyghurs, the cabin announcements are made only in Chinese and English.

There are many more areas in the cultural inheritance sphere that cause unhappiness, and these often manifest themselves in ethnic conflicts. The crux of the problem is that ethnic regional autonomy is still not truly being implemented, and neither is respect for culture or religion. The Xinjiang problem is first and foremost a problem of the overall system. Obviously, no matter whether you're solving the "Xinjiang Problem" or the "Tibet Problem," you can only do so gradually by changing the unreasonable system. Fundamentally, it depends on political reform. But, looking at the current situation, I haven't seen any signs of courage on the part of the government or preparations for carrying forward such reform.

Clearly, if the Chinese government had followed through on its legal and political promises to the XUAR, the situation would be much better now. Autonomy for China's ethnic regions hasn't been truly implemented and there are many problems with the protection of the Uyghur people's rights to cultural, linguistic, and religious freedom, as well as other rights guaranteed to citizens.

Of course, I don't think that you can fundamentally solve these problems through modernizing the region; it could only help a bit to ease some of Uyghurs' unhappiness over the rule of the CCP secretaries. This is because in these two regions, economic growth is always accompanied by a heavy influx of Han migrants. (Don't forget that for a long time this sort of migration was a product of political mobilization, not spurred by industrialization, urbanization, or commercialization. Of course, the effect of these factors becomes more salient every day.) This influx of Han migrants leads to even more inequality and increased marginalization of Uyghurs. The Uyghur people aren't willing to give up their freedom and accept marginalization in exchange for regional GDP growth and economic prosperity. You therefore can't assume that economic growth will lead to ethnic harmony. Many signs show that the accumulated feelings of ethnic grievance in Xinjiang have already reached a new and more serious level.

I want to ask people like Ma Rong: Given that the policies and institutions of autonomy in Xinjiang have never really been implemented, why is the solution to get rid of ethnic regional autonomy? If Uyghurs and Tibetans have the need and determination to preserve their ethnic culture, history, and religion, and they have the right under Chinese law to enjoy ethnic regional autonomy, then what reason is there to abolish their right to ethnic autonomy?

I feel that, on the contrary, the problem is not with ethnic autonomy itself but rather with the fact that ethnic autonomy hasn't been implemented. The core problem is not that the vast majority of Uyghurs want independence. Only a very small minority believe that Xinjiang independence is the only way to solve the problem. Most Uyghurs accept China's sovereignty over Xinjiang; they simply seek a truly meaningful kind of autonomy.

The "cultural" and "political" transformations proposed by Ma Rong are not the correct categories to be guiding ethnic policy. Ethnic regional autonomy and preferential policies are the current choice for resolving ethnic problems. We currently need to focus not on whether to keep policies like ethnic regional autonomy but on how to overcome institutional obstacles or systemic problems in order to improve and implement these policies. Practice demonstrates that the policy of autonomy faces all sorts of complex problems, but the costs are too high for us to conclude that the current theory guiding ethnic affairs is outdated and that we need to reinvent the wheel.

In theory, we should not only take another look at the accomplishments and experience of others; it's even more important to truly implement all of the ethnic policies and the ethnic autonomy system. If we simply treat the symptoms of the problem reactively, there will be no future. Ethnic problems are always incredibly thorny in every country, whether democratic or not. There's no perfect model to resolve and eliminate ethnic problems.

China's theory of ethnic relations is out of date, that's for sure. But you can't simply conclude that it ought to be tossed into the dustbin of history. The United States is a multiethnic country made up of immigrants, whereas China is a country where different ethnic groups have lived alongside each other for generations. The ethnic problems faced by each country are fundamentally different. I don't completely approve of the "cultural transformation" of minority groups in the United States; the ethnic problems you see there aren't any better than ours. The United States has deeply rooted ethnic problems, such as the problems of American Indian reservations or the systematic marginalization of urban African Americans. However, correct values about racial equality can be promoted through the American media and other means. After incidents occur, the media, politicians, and police officials can all reflect and reconsider and express their views about the incidents without inflaming racial feelings.

In practice, we urgently need to develop a new way of thinking about ethnicity. Simply changing our methods and emphasizing "diversity in unity" (for example, the cultural and ethnic transformation of all minorities) would still reflect a political arrangement of centrality and consolidated marginality. And it would still lack a strong-enough explanation about what makes China an integrated whole.

In the savage era, when you conquered another people you would employ a unifying policy of eliminating their culture. China now uses this argument to refute the Western media. The ancestors of modern Westerners truly did some bad things, but as an emerging great power of the twenty-first century, China mustn't follow the old colonial path. We should do much better in our treatment of different peoples and cultures.

Uyghurs, Tibetans, and many others are watching the Chinese government. If it can resolve the Xinjiang and Tibet problems in an appropriate and wise way, it would surely cause the world to see the Chinese people in a new light. The series of incidents in Xinjiang demonstrates that accumulated ethnic grievances have reached a new and even more serious level. The threat that once was deliberately exaggerated may now be turning into reality.

The task at hand should be to grant the Uyghur people their legal right to ethnic autonomy, give them an opportunity to equal development, eliminate corruption, prohibit expressions of Han chauvinism that denigrate Uyghurs, and implement the rule of law. According to our policies on ethnic regional autonomy and the provisions of our constitution, we should have responsibility for deciding all public matters large and small having to do with our own autonomous region.

So, can we implement the institutions and policies of the regional autonomy system? Uyghurs are asking: Isn't it time to rethink Xinjiang's ethnic policies?

The repeated ethnic riots of 2008 are now part of history. Many people are concerned about how the central government will adjust future ethnic policies. At the very least, the main status of ethnic regional autonomy cannot be changed. Neither Tibetan independence nor Xinjiang independence can be considered among the world's most serious separatist movements. You therefore cannot say that ethnic autonomy is a mistake because of such movements. Establishing a system of academic reflection and introspection is what's most needed. This reflection goes both ways, for both the Han (government) and the Uyghurs. Only intellectuals have enough space and enough frankness to do this kind of rethinking. Only when there is a civic education truly beneficial to all of China can adjustment of ethnic policies get underway. How much longer do we have to wait for such rethinking to begin?

A Case Study: Cadre Language

Many ethnic cadres were recruited and trained in the 1960s. Why can't even one be found to serve as party secretary of the XUAR? Even though the party has groomed many ethnic cadres, it still sees their ethnic difference as a source of different thinking and believes that they can't be trusted. Don't you think that the ethnic population experiences this same sort of distrust as well?

Many measures have been adopted to restrict Uyghur culture and religion, including replacement of the Uyghur language with Chinese in primary schools. Of course Uyghurs will resent this type of restriction. Let me give you a clear example using language, which plays a hugely important part in daily life. Han make up 90 percent of the Chinese population, so their Chinese language has been established as the official language. That of course makes sense. Actually, Uyghurs understand that if you can't speak Chinese well you'll encounter many difficulties in the rest of China. They don't argue with that.

Now the problem is that large numbers of Han have come to Xinjiang, and they play leading roles in most institutions. Many recruitment notices in Xinjiang state clearly that only Han need apply. If Uyghurs feel that they are being marginalized in their own homeland and that they've become a minority, of course it's going to lead to strong feelings of unhappiness.

This is a problem that many other people have a difficult time understanding. Your average Han feels that they have a right to go anywhere they like—after all, Xinjiang is part of China. They feel that they've come and worked hard and that they've made the local economy more prosperous—what's wrong with that? The problem they don't recognize is the effect their actions have on others, particularly in terms of how it makes them feel.

My Ideals and the Career Path
I Have Chosen

This essay is dated January 17, 2011. It is unclear where it was first published, though at one point it was widely available on Chinese-language websites.

1. My upbringing and my ideals

I was born in 1969 into a Uyghur family in Atush City, Kizilsu Kirghiz Autonomous Prefecture, Xinjiang Uyghur Autonomous Region (XUAR). I grew up in a government employee residential compound where Uyghurs and Han lived together. My grandfather's generation was illiterate, but my father was among the first generation of educated Uyghurs brought up in New China. At the end of the 1950s, after my father graduated from middle school, he was sent to the interior of China for college. He studied at the Central University for Nationalities [now Minzu University], Beijing Normal University, and Lanzhou Railway Institute. After graduation, he worked at the Southern Xinjiang People's Liberation Army (PLA) military zone, and then as a civilian. In 1971, at the age of twenty-eight, my father died tragically during the Cultural Revolution. I was two, and my little brother was only eleven months old. It was my mother who raised the four of us, my brothers and me, while doing auto repair work in Atush. Today, most of my father's colleagues have become XUAR-level cadres. The older generation has kept silent about the past, and I do not understand the complicated politics of that time. As a result, while we are proud of our father, I don't really know what kind of a person he was and how he died.

In 1980, my eldest brother joined the army at age fifteen, but he soon left the army and pursued studies in universities in Shanghai, Urumqi, Dalian, and Beijing. As a cadre, he served as secretary of the Atush Communist Youth League, chief of the Personnel Office of the Organization Department of Kizilsu Kirghiz Autonomous Prefecture, secretary of the Kizilsu Kirghiz Prefecture Communist Youth League, chief of the Kizilsu Kirghiz Prefecture Administrative Bureau, and chief of the Civil Affairs Bureau of the Kizilsu Kirghiz Prefecture. Currently he is the Communist Party secretary of the Transportation Bureau of Kizilsu Kirghiz Prefecture and a member of the Kizilsu Kirghiz People's Political Consultative Conference (CPPCC).

My second older brother has worked in the public security system for many years now. He was once the youngest captain of the criminal investigation squad [in the prefecture], and now he is the secretary of the Disciplinary Inspection Committee of the Kizilsu Kirghiz Prefecture Public Security Bureau, as well as a member of the bureau's CCP committee. Aside from my two brothers, my sister-in-law (the wife of my second older brother) and my brothers' children also work in the public security system. To a degree, my family is actually a family in the public security system, although, because of me, they have all been implicated in recent years.

In 1985, I was admitted at age sixteen to study in the interior of China. I left my hometown to undertake pre-undergraduate studies at Minzu University, undergraduate studies in the Geography Department of Northeast Normal University, and graduate study for a master's degree at Minzu University's Institute of Economic Research. My academic career was deeply influenced by Professors Shi Zheng Yi, Chen Cai, and Zhang Kewu. I will never in my life forget the lessons that they imparted upon me as a Uyghur youth, nor will I forget their genuine interest in, and concerns about, Xinjiang and Uyghur society, as well as their academic integrity.

In 1991, after I graduated from college, I was employed by Minzu University; for a time I was secretary of the department's Communist Youth League. In 1994, I transferred to Minzu University's Institute of Economic Research, where I taught development economics, advanced foreign economics, and the economics of the Xinjiang region. In 1996, I studied abroad in Korea at my own expense. In 2001, I was an exchange scholar at the Pakistan National Development Research Institute through a joint China–Pakistan cultural exchange program to research on the security environment and economic development in Xinjiang and surrounding areas. In 2003, I became a faculty member at the International Trade Department of College of Economics at Minzu University. I have since taught many courses, such as International Trade Affairs, International Settlements and Credit, Strategic Research on Sustainable Development of Xinjiang's Population, Resources and Environment, and Politics, Economics, Society and Culture in Central Asia.

Around 1994, I developed an intense interest in the economic and social issues Xinjiang faces. In addition to publishing articles in the *Guangming Daily*, *Economic Information Daily*, and *Western Development Paper*, I also published over twenty articles in academic periodicals, including the *Journal of Minzu University*; the *Journal of Research on Education for Ethnic Minorities*; *Tribune of Social Sciences in Xinjiang*; *National Economy*; and the *Journal of Kashgar Teachers College*. As early as in 1994, I proposed setting up a special economic zone in Kashgar in southern Xinjiang. In order to expand the horizons of my professional research, I have been studying English. I have also taught myself basic Korean, Japanese, Urdu, and Russian, and can conduct simple conversation and access information in these languages.

Outside of my work, in my spare time I engaged in business and had pretty good results in the stock market and joint venture projects. For a time, when I was restricted from teaching, my friends even suggested that I make a complete switch and become a businessman. However, having witnessed a great number of cases of ethnic conflict and killing, political unrest, and failed social transformation during my extensive travels throughout Central Asia, Russia, and South Asia, my desire grew stronger and stronger to completely devote my energies to researching Xinjiang and Central Asian issues, so that tragedies such as those abroad won't take place in China.

To this end, I have personally funded and conducted large-scale social surveys. I simultaneously took time to study sociology, ethnology, and geopolitics by taking classes or through self-instruction. Such endeavors have expanded my horizons beyond economics and provided me with other perspectives and analytical tools. Aside from studying failed cases from the former Soviet Union as well as Eastern Europe, I have also looked at some successful cases to see how developed countries such as the United States as well as those in Europe have handled and resolved ethnic issues and social issues. My hope is that such comparative examinations will provide abundant lessons for endeavors undertaken in China.

I love my mother deeply, who suffered great hardships in raising me. I love my still-impoverished and long-suffering ethnic group. I love this land, which has nurtured me. I earnestly hope my homeland can become as prosperous and developed as the interior of China. I worry about my homeland and my country falling into turmoil and division. I hope that China, having endured many misfortunes, will become a great nation of harmonious inter-ethnic coexistence and develop a splendid civilization. I will devote myself to Xinjiang's social, economic, and cultural development, to inter-ethnic under-standing, and to finding the way to achieve harmonious ethnic coexistence amid the social transformation today. These are my ideals and personal objectives, and the choices I have made have their roots in my family's history, my upbringing, my mother's teachings, and my education, as well as personal experiences.

2. I am an academic dedicated to researching Xinjiang issues and Central Asian sociology, economics, and geopolitics. Although some people today continue to describe me as a political figure, or hope that I will become one, from the start I have maintained that I am only a scholar, and harbor neither the intention nor the desire to be politicized. Outside of my scholarship, I wish to be known solely as an emissary and a conduit helping to make connections and promoting ethnic exchange and communication.

Since 1994, due to my frequent and blunt criticism of failures of the local government in Xinjiang, [authorities have] constantly interfered with my teaching. Since 1999, I have had no opportunities to publish any articles. From 1999 to 2003, I was barred from teaching at Minzu University, where I had been employed.

In recent years, following my growing research and investigation into Xinjiang's problems, and after I had set up the Chinese-language Uyghur Online website, pressure has mounted not only on my professional life, but also on my relatives in Xinjiang. They have often bitterly entreated me in the hope that I will speak out less, mind my own business, and focus on making money. Meanwhile, I can see that Xinjiang's ethnic problems are increasingly grave and that inter-ethnic hatred has escalated.

I know very well that there are not many people from our ethnic group who, like me, have enjoyed a quality education and have had ample opportunities and gained broad experience. Similarly, few people in China possess the same natural advantages that I do with regard to Xinjiang issues and Central Asian issues. In this field, few scholars possess great insights or a sense of responsibility. Yet the challenges facing Chinese society are so difficult that I cannot rightly dismiss the responsibility to pursue what I believe is the most meaningful career.

However, the call of duty implicates my family, which causes me great suffering.

After the tragedy on July 5, 2009, the world suddenly paid attention to Xinjiang issues. I too attracted widespread attention and was inevitably treated as a political figure. I do not reject any person or group's interest in Xinjiang issues, but I have always endeavored to avoid being treated as a political symbol in any way, even when it is well intentioned.

It is my belief that I will not be doing a service to my ethnic group and my country unless I remain a scholar—and a "clean" one at that—and use my free time to help others and serve the public interest.

Precisely because of this strong belief, since July 5, 2009, I have doggedly refused to take a single cent from foreign organizations, whether diplomatic entities or NGOs, when I encountered financial difficulties resulting from external pressure. Even during business dealings, I was unwilling to make any money through foreign connections. I could have sat at home and made money from my political and economic contacts in Central Asia, Europe, and America. If I were a Han, maybe I could have profited in this way, but as someone who has been under suspicion, I have to maintain even stricter standards for myself, bearing more pressure and facing more trials than Han intellectuals could possibly imagine.

Because of the sensitive nature of ethnic issues, for a long time there has existed not only social divisions between Han and Uyghur people, but also a lack of regular communication between Han and Uyghur intellectuals. This division, as well as mutual suspicions, has worsened the ethnic situation. Yet, amazingly, there have been almost no public discussions about it, and the atmosphere around it is both strange and terrifying.

As a result, I founded the Uyghur Online website at the end of 2005 to provide Uyghurs and Han with a platform for discussion and exchange. Of course, I knew that there would be an intense clash of opinions, but I believe that confronting differences is not frightening. What is truly frightening are silenced suspicions and hatred.

After founding Uyghur Online, I began to make an effort to interact with Han intellectuals in order to bring Xinjiang issues to their attention, thus allowing them to contribute their valuable perspectives and experiences to the discussion, and to introduce them to Uyghur culture and society.

The July 5 tragedy—and Xinjiang's ethnic relations in its aftermath—made it clear to me that ethnic hatred and suspicion had built up alarmingly. To thaw that hatred and suspicion, I came up with the idea of a grassroots National Harmony Day (or National Reconciliation Day), held on July 5, to commemorate the tragedy. It would take advantage of the summer holiday and allow [groups of] two families of different ethnicities to send their children to live in the other's home. This would hopefully build inter-ethnic emotional ties and friendship and also serve to cultivate a sense of inclusiveness, understanding, and respect for different cultures. But the idea was aborted due to various external factors.

From the beginning, it was a rational idea born out of my education and training that ethnic relations should be built through reasonable, patient, tolerant, and moderate approaches that respect history and reality and focus on the future. As I have practiced it over time, such an attitude has grown to be a natural feeling of mine.

As a university professor, I have the strong desire to share my views, hopes, and methodology with my students. Unlike a lot of teachers, I diligently prepare handouts and lesson plans for each class, and for a long time I have offered open and voluntary classes on Xinjiang issues on Saturdays.

I encouraged more Uyghur students to pursue studies in sociology, law, economics, political science, anthropology, and other fields so that in making career choices they will be able to combine their personal goals with the progress of their ethnic group as well as their country. These subjects provide a systematic methodology, and can transform emotional energy and visceral enthusiasm for ethnic issues into a rational and scientific approach. The cultivation of such an approach is certainly rare among the Uyghurs, and therefore precious; but even in China as a whole there is far from enough of it.

3. I have maintained a long-term and sustained interest in Xinjiang and Central Asian issues. With regard to Xinjiang, this entails social, economic, and cultural development; inter-ethnic interaction; as well as the balance between sovereignty, unity, and local autonomy under China's current conditions in an era of transformation.

People in Xinjiang today generally look back nostalgically at ethnic relations during the planned economy era [1949–76] as well as Hu Yaobang and Song Hanliang era [1976–89]. During the planned economy era, the government distributed resources equally and fairly, creating a positive sense of equality among ethnic groups. In addition, at that time the population was restricted in mobility and there were few opportunities for group comparisons that could result in a sense of inequality. During the Hu Yaobang and Song Hanliang era, the political climate was relaxed. On the surface more people seemed to be voicing discontent publicly, but people trusted each other and felt least suppressed, and social synergy was the strongest.

Since the 1990s, rapid marketization in Xinjiang has produced a great deal of economic development. Unequal development opportunities among ethnic groups have grown more apparent. Certain developments within Uyghur communities have been particularly worrying. Theft, pickpocketing, drug trafficking, drug abuse, and prostitution—vices against which a devoutly religious people as the Uyghurs are supposed to have natural resistance—have gotten so bad that our entire ethnic group is suddenly perceived as a crime-prone community. The Uyghurs have fallen mercilessly into the fate of the "Malthusian trap."

At the same time, these serious social problems have become a forbidden subject for study, creating a discursive void. Few dare to touch upon these problems directly, let alone conduct systematic social investigations and analyses in search of solutions. On the one hand, the Uyghurs' social problems lead to increasing dissatisfaction and distrust of the government and of Han people; on the other, discriminatory ideas against the Uyghur people among members of Han society—especially in the interior of China—grow deeper.

As a Uyghur intellectual, I strongly sense that the great rift of distrust between the Uyghur and Han societies is getting worse each day, especially within the younger generation. Unemployment and discrimination along ethnic lines have caused widespread animosity. The discord did not explode and dissipate along with the July 5th Incident and during subsequent social interactions. Instead, it has started to build up once again.

The situation is getting gradually worse. Yet fewer and fewer people dare to speak out. Since 1997, the primary government objective in the region has been to combat the "three evil forces" [terrorism, separatism, and religious extremism]. Its indirect effect is that Uyghur cadres and intellectuals feel strongly distrusted and the political atmosphere is oppressive.

As a Uyghur scholar living in Beijing, where the legal environment is relatively better, I have a duty—one which I cannot rightly dismiss—to focus my attention on Xinjiang's problems. This has always required not only knowledge and training, but above all courage.

The outbreak of the July 5th unrest in 2009 and, before it, the March 14th Incident in Lhasa, Tibet, in 2008, clearly reminds us that as China is undergoing rapid changes, it is an extremely urgent task to explore how to achieve ethnic harmony. China is accustomed to the use of political solutions, especially those employing the use of political indoctrination. Rarely do such discussions seek to improve laws and regulations, as well as the art of politics, to foster an environment suitable for ethnic harmony. Virtually no one in China works on the technical aspect of harmonious ethnic relations—even the awareness of it is absent.

No good political intentions or political desires can be divorced from the meticulous and thorough technical designs that support them. In China especially, the government is accustomed to large-scale government-directed organization and mobilization of social resources without regard for the costs, rather than long-term and patient technical arrangements. Looking at the examples of multiethnic diversity in Malaysia and Singapore, we can see that a technically meticulous, even-handed management of ethnic interests produces ethnic tolerance and harmonious relations. That's why I have always believed in the importance of my own endeavors.

As ethnic issues in China become more sensitive and pressing, more and more studies are examining China's ethnic policies from the perspective of combating separatism, drawing lessons from countries with failed ethnic policies. However, most of these studies have a strongly Han-centered ideology and focus on how to establish control. Consequently, they actually defend and endorse the approach of failed local-government ethnic policies (even when they seem to be criticizing them). In foreign countries, there are many cases whereby states successfully resolved or mitigated ethnic conflicts and defused crises caused by ethnic division. However, these aforementioned Chinese studies have taken none of these successes into consideration. I am deeply worried about this academic tendency, which misleads policymakers.

My research on Central Asia reflects my own personal interests and my connection to the region. As a natural extension of Xinjiang issues, I must pay attention to the social, political, economic, and cultural trends in Central Asian countries: not only do Central Asia and Xinjiang share vast borders, but they also belong to the same linguistic, cultural, and religious family. Situated along a multiethnic border, Xinjiang can be affected by a slight change in the greater region.

Furthermore, from a geostrategic perspective, China must research how to effectively exert influence in the political, economic, and cultural spheres of Central Asia, not only so that it can benefit from an enhanced regional security environment, but also so that both China and Central Asia can build stronger, mutually beneficial relations. This is another aspect of my interests in the region.

I have continued to gain knowledge because of my language skills, and I have established wide contacts in local governments and business circles of the region through my travels. On top of that, I also have had successful business experiences. These are all areas in which I differ from Chinese researchers on Central Asia. It is easier for me to obtain local approval when exploring Central Asian problems because of my background and also because of my access to resources and information.

With these advantages, I have been able to successfully facilitate investment by many Han businessmen into Central Asia, and I have also served as a middleman to assist state-owned enterprises like Petro China and Sino Pec, resolving all sorts of troubles and problems, so that they can expand into local markets there.

I deeply believe that the question of how China exerts influence in Central Asia has neither been analyzed carefully nor considered as a whole. China should play a more active and effective role in Central Asia.

4. Uyghur Online is a website I personally founded to help all ethnic groups in China—as well as the world—understand Xinjiang and the Uyghurs. Conversely, the website seeks to allow ethnic groups living in Xinjiang to understand the world. Thus it promotes mutual understanding as well as dialogue among ethnic communities. It is managed to prevent any pro-independence, separatist, or irresponsible inflammatory postings, and it does not post anything subversive.

I founded Uyghur Online because I discovered that many websites and search portals contained a large amount of posts that incited hatred and attacked the Uyghur community. As a result, I strongly felt that deep division existed between the Uyghur and

Han peoples due to a lack of mutual understanding. But there was no platform for communication and dialogue. Han and Uyghur netizens have been talking past each other, with no opportunities to exchange views one-on-one and listen meaningfully to each other.

Moreover, many people in Chinese society discuss the Uyghur people, but not many people possess a basic knowledge of Uyghur society. In a multiethnic society, such circumstances are undesirable. Since no one else was doing it, I thought I would fill this gap.

Uyghur Online is managed to prevent any pro-independence, separatist, or irresponsible inflammatory postings, and it does not post subversive materials. However, it does not forbid posts that expose social ills in Xinjiang or elsewhere, so long as they show good intentions and the content is authentic.

As expected, nationalistic Hans and Uyghurs have had heated arguments on the forum. Nevertheless, I have always maintained that one should not fear differences of opinion and opposition, but rather, [fear only] not having opportunities for exchange. As long as there is exchange, there will be consensus. In reality, although some Han netizens have criticized my comments as drastic or unjust, I have also earned the respect of many of them: I don't agree with your views, but I understand that you are well-meaning.

Uyghur Online is both a platform for exchanging views as well as a platform for performing acts of public service. In recent years, criminals have abducted, lured, or kidnapped Uyghur children and brought them to the interior of China, where their pickpocketing is increasingly a serious social problem. It disturbs local people's sense of security and also damages the reputation of the entire ethnic community. Although just about everyone knows about this social issue and it has drawn growing attention, not a single media outlet has dared to discuss it because it is deemed too sensitive. No organization or agency has dared to attempt to systematically address the problem. Each child is a treasure of the nation and [represents] the future of society, regardless of his or her ethnicity.

For this reason, I set up a platform on Uyghur Online to aid vagrant Uyghur children, to actively reach out to local civic anticrime organizations, and to offer aid and legal support to vagrant children. This led to a *Phoenix Weekly* report about the matter, which then led the Xinjiang government to begin putting assistance for vagrant children on its official agenda.

In addition, I made Uyghur Online a tool to influence and solicit Uyghurs' ideas about society. In Uyghur society today, there are virtually no rational, moderate, and constructive voices that grapple with the real problems of Uyghur society, free of [China's] official, orthodox, and constrained propaganda. From overseas there are no lack of provocative and subversive statements, which don't solve any real problems. As Xinjiang faces the danger of escalating ethnic conflicts, and discussions of ethnic problems tend to be radical, I believe that one of our most important tasks is for us to use rational and constructive voices to compete against more extreme ones in the marketplace of ideas, moving social sentiments in a more positive direction.

Because Uyghur Online is independent and unique in Uyghur society, it has gradually gained recognition and influence, and its ongoing debates have allowed more people to recognize the role it plays. However, over the course of running the website, I have been under enormous pressure. The website was repeatedly forced to close or has fallen victim to unwarranted attacks. I have been regularly summoned and warned [by the government] but continued the website anyway, believing that Uyghur Online is of irreplaceable value and that I am doing the right thing.

Conclusion

As a Uyghur intellectual, I naturally have deep feelings for my ethnic group, and I feel uneasy about its impoverishment and its many sufferings attributable to historical and circumstantial factors. I have equally deep feelings for my country, and, having traveled to dozens of other countries, I have come to the conclusion that national pride runs deep within my veins. The pain and pride experienced by both my ethnic group and also my countrymen are my own pain and my own pride.

Today in Xinjiang and elsewhere, we are witnessing a unique period where ethnic issues are of unprecedented importance and difficulty. Whether rationally or emotionally, I cannot accept any part of the nation being separated. With regard to ethnic issues, I do not oppose the natural fusing of ethnic groups, because it reflects a natural as well as a social law. Historically, both the Han and Uyghur ethnicities are products of multiethnic mingling. However, I do oppose a false and calculated ethnic harmony. Use of administrative means to keep ethnic groups together is, in essence, a use of force that breeds division, whereas tolerance as a means to encourage diversity will lead to mutual harmony and unity.

We can solve ethnic problems only by exploring ethnic autonomy and making China a multiethnic, multicultural, and attractive country.

In terms of governance in China today, our multiethnic and multicultural reality has complicated the issues and problems of this era of social transformation. Even so, with regard to culture and creativity, this diversity is an invaluable source of wealth benefiting all ethnic groups. Whether looking vertically at Chinese history or horizontally at the world today, it's clear that the greater a country's cultural diversity and tolerance, the greater its creativity.

Any thinking that doggedly stresses a particular group's cultural uniqueness and superiority, thus making it noninclusive, is closed-minded and a thing of the past. It will inevitably kill the culture it means to enshrine and protect.

In China's constitution, provisions governing ethnic autonomy provide a good framework for coexistence and the development of a multiethnic culture. But in practice, we need to explore how to better implement it through laws and regulations. We should take the initiative to learn from the successful experiences of other countries to fashion a suitable model for China.

I firmly believe that as long as we have the wisdom and vision for the future, as well as the courage to face reality head-on, China will be able to find a path to ethnic autonomy that achieves an ideal balance between the integrity of a unified nation and ethnic autonomy.

Although in recent years I have been restricted from going to Xinjiang, I deeply believe that the huge amounts of progress and changes that have occurred in China, which I have seen with my own eyes in the last few decades, will not stop. I strongly believe that my efforts and inquiries will become part of China's progress, and I will be very proud of what I have done.

"The Wounds of the Uyghur People Have Not Healed"

Open letter to China's State Council and the National People's Congress, published online on July 5, 2013.

Today is the fourth anniversary of the July 5th Incident, which has caused severe psychological trauma both to Uyghurs and to Han Chinese. Uyghur blood flows in my veins, and I grew up in the embrace of a Uyghur family. I have made a long-term study of the issues facing Xinjiang and, as an independent intellectual, constantly make suggestions and recommendations to the government. I carry an unavoidable responsibility both to my people and to my country for the correct handling of ethnic relations.

Over the past four years, the psychological wounds of the Uyghur people have not healed. On the contrary, salt has been rubbed into them. There is continual and constant oppression of Uyghurs. One example is the disappearances of Uyghurs following the July 5th Incident. Out of 18,000 people detained in the wake of July 5, 2009, some have been sentenced to death, some have been sentenced to jail, and some have been released. However, there is still a group that has "disappeared." I would like therefore to offer some suggestions on the matter of the "disappeared."

Following investigations by our website, Uyghur Online, and by other independent media outlets, we have been able to confirm the identities of thirty-four of the "disappeared" Uyghurs:

1. Imam Mamatli
2. Abahun Sopur

3. Turghun Obulqasim
4. Tursunjan Toxti
5. Zaker Mamat
6. Muhter Mehat
7. Mamatabdulla Abdurahim
8. Abudureyim Sidiq
9. Alim Abudureyim
10. Alimjan Helaji
11. Mamat Barat
12. Ayitghazi Hasanbek
13. Amantaj Jumataj
14. Yusup Turghun
15. Memtimin Yasin
16. Eysajan Emat
17. Jumajan
18. Bekri
19. Abdughani Ezim
20. Abdusamat Abulait
21. Nabijan
22. Akber Tursun
23. Tursunjan Tohti
24. Abdulaziz Ablat
25. Ematjan Juma
26. Turdimamat Tursunniyaz
27. Abukerim Abla
28. Imin Momin
29. Tayirjan Ebay
30. Abdurahim Qadir
31. Alimjan Bakri
32. Alimjan Sulayman
33. Toxtiali Hashim
34. Abliz Qadir

At first, the families of missing persons waited for the government to explain the situation, but no news came. By the following year, some of the parents of missing persons (Patigul Ghulam, Qurbangul Mijit, Barat Haji, and others) began to petition the authorities in Beijing.

But a few days later, local police and officials followed them and forced them to return home. In the third year, they began to give interviews to the foreign media, making accusations against the government. According to foreign media reports, the identities of thirty-seven of the missing Uyghurs [and Kazakhs] have been confirmed from information received directly from the families of the missing. There is evidence that thirty-four of those were arrested by the police, while there is no evidence in the case of the other three.

The stories of what happened during their arrest, and of their families' attempts to track them down, have already been made public to the world. To date, there have been more than seventy news reports, ten statements, and a published report, including the names of the disappeared, their and their families' photographs, and the details of their arrests and disappearances, some of which have been confirmed by police and officials. I think we can say that the question of these disappearances is no longer a secret to the international community, still less among Uyghurs.

Currently, the families of missing persons are receiving only the following minimalistic and evasive replies:

"We are continuing to look for them."

"The investigation has ended, and we need to wait for orders from higher up before we can announce the findings."

"Your [son or daughter] has escaped from prison, and we do not know his [her] whereabouts."

"Your [son or daughter] has been released, and may have fled the country."

Obviously, it is not an accountable government that gives such replies to the families of missing persons.

Officials of the Xinjiang Uyghur Autonomous Region government, Urumqi municipal police department, and local levels of government often pass the buck when contacted by families trying to find missing persons. Families of missing persons are kept shuttling between the three departments, causing them great emotional damage and considerable financial loss. Some relatives have been placed under surveillance and detained after looking for missing persons. For example, Patigul Ghulam, the mother of disappeared person Imam Mamatli, was detained for seven days.

The identities of these thirty-seven missing persons have been confirmed only because their families had the courage to come forward and report them, and because they have been reported in the foreign media. There may be many more yet to be revealed. But even if these thirty-seven people are the only ones about whom their families can't get news, this is still no small matter.

The authorities have yet to give a clear explanation to the families of missing persons, who may well have died in prison. It is unsurprising that reports about the missing have been exaggerated by some foreign organizations, who claim the number is in the tens of thousands. There are a variety of theories about the missing even within the Uyghur community. This leads to great disappointment in the government among the Uyghurs, and even to a psychology of hatred, which is an understandable phenomenon.

There may be various reasons for the government's attitude on this issue. But I cannot understand why the government does not inform the families of the whereabouts of these disappeared people, because its duty is to safeguard national stability and security.

Perhaps the authorities fear that announcing the fate of the missing will lead to social unrest or damage the image of the government. But I do not think this concern is justified. If there has been a dereliction of duty by officials, then the government should investigate and bring to justice those responsible. This would not only prove that there is the rule of law in our country, it would help heal more than 10 million psychological wounds among Uyghurs and help restore their trust in the state.

Hiding the situation of these missing people isn't a long-term solution. Sooner or later, the truth will be revealed to the world. Currently the majority of families of disappeared persons have asked the government to provide the whereabouts of the missing. They say that if it is determined that these missing family members have died, they will be able to hold a funeral for the dead, submit to fate, and come to peace of mind through prayers for the dead. If the government were to apologize to the families of missing persons and provide full compensation to their families, I believe this would also be acceptable. At the very least, it would dampen current discontent directed toward the government.

To this end, I propose the following recommendations:

The government should publish independent, comprehensive, detailed, and persuasive reports on the disappearance of Uyghurs [and Kazakhs] following the July 5th Incident.

The state should issue an apology and compensation to the victims' families, so as to ease their psychological suffering.

Those responsible for any wrongful deaths should be brought to justice.

I have repeatedly made known my observations and recommendations regarding Xinjiang, which has brought me a great deal of trouble and "tea-drinking" [with the state security police]. Making these proposals may result in even more "tea-drinking." But it makes me happy, because I believe that many others would like to suggest the same thing, and because I am telling the truth.

Essay

Present-Day Ethnic Problems in Xinjiang Uyghur Autonomous Region: Overview and Recommendations

This article, a total of 24,000 characters in Chinese, was first posted on the Daxiong Gonghui website sometime after Ilham Tohti's arrest in January 2014. Daxiong Gonghui described the origin of the article in a note: "This document was written by Ilham Tohti, Associate Professor of Economics at Minzu University of China (formerly Central Nationalities University), in response to a 2011 request from high-level officials in the Chinese government. Ilham Tohti made first-draft revisions to this document in October of 2013, but was unable to complete a final draft." The post has since been censored and is only available elsewhere as reposts.

Since Zhang Chunxian took office, a big push on Xinjiang policy by the Chinese central government and a series of initiatives by Zhang Chunxian himself have rekindled hope in Xinjiang for the region's future social stability and development prospects.[1] Furthermore, Zhang Chunxian has managed, in a very short period of time, to win high praise from local ethnic minority officials and intellectuals alike.

At present, the new administration in Xinjiang is relying on increased economic investment and improvement in citizens' livelihoods to quell ethnic tensions. These policies will likely

---

1 In April 2010, Zhang Chunxian was appointed Communist Party secretary of the Xinjiang Uyghur Autonomous Region, replacing Wang Lequan, whose divisive policies may have helped to fuel ethnic unrest in the region. Zhang Chunxian's appointment was regarded by many as a positive step toward defusing ethnic tensions in Xinjiang.—Editors

have a positive short-term effect, but because they do not address deep-seated problems, we cannot afford to be sanguine about Xinjiang's future, nor can we be certain that violence will not erupt again. If the government is to win broad-based popular support and achieve genuine long-term peace and stability, it must promote further systemic and social adjustments.

To this end, I have prepared a simple list of nine issues affecting ethnic relations in Xinjiang. For each, I have included an overview of the present situation, causes and contributing factors, and proposed solutions.

I. Unemployment among Ethnic Minorities

Overview

Unemployment is a social issue that affects all regions of China, but Xinjiang's unemployment problem tends to be concentrated among ethnic minorities. For Uyghurs who migrate to the cities in search of work, employment opportunities are markedly limited, confined to a narrow band of service-industry jobs, mostly jobs in restaurants. There is a vast gap in employment opportunities available to different ethnic groups: Uyghur and other ethnic-minority job applicants face significant employment discrimination. These factors in turn fuel resentment toward the government and toward the Han Chinese majority.

Because the factors driving urban and rural unemployment are so different, we can divide the employment issue in Xinjiang into two distinct facets: (1) unemployment among Uyghur university graduates and (2) the rural labor surplus.

1. Unemployment among Uyghur university graduates

According to official government data, only 17 percent of ethnic Uyghur university students in Xinjiang manage to secure a full-time job by the time they graduate. This is far below the rate for ethnic Han Chinese university students. My own research reveals that the actual job placement rate for Uyghur university students approaching graduation is even lower, at less than 15 percent. The difficulty of finding work after graduation not only impoverishes ethnic-minority families who have sacrificed to send their children to university, it also contributes to the notion, widespread among Uyghurs, that education is useless.

2. The rural labor surplus

The rural labor surplus in Xinjiang is a serious problem. The root cause of this excess rural labor force is lagging urbanization and industrialization in Uyghur areas. In fact, the actual urbanization rate among the Uyghur population is only about 10 percent.

Most of Xinjiang's Uyghur population is concentrated in the rural south, where the average amount of arable land per capita is less than one *mu*, or one-sixth of an acre. This sort of marginal existence and inescapable poverty not only bottles up vast reserves of surplus rural labor, it also gives rise to lawlessness and criminal behavior, making these areas potential breeding grounds for future threats to the social order. If this vicious cycle is allowed to continue, it may even bring about the collapse of southern Xinjiang's fragile oasis ecosystem.

Causes

1. Given the absence or nonenforcement of national ethnic policies, the primary cause of employment difficulties among minority university students is blatant ethnic discrimination in hiring. Ethnic minorities are severely under-recruited for jobs in the civil service and in state-owned enterprises. Prior to the July 2009 ethnic unrest in Urumqi, many private-sector job advertisements openly stated that only Han Chinese applicants would be considered; some state-owned enterprises went so far as to recruit Han Chinese from other parts of mainland China,

rather than hire local ethnic minorities. At some workplaces with no Uyghur employees, Uyghurs may be stopped by security guards and prevented from entering the premises. Severely curtailed employment prospects have given rise to an unusual phenomenon in Xinjiang: a craze for extra-curricular foreign language training courses. Xinjiang's ethnic minority university students are keener on studying foreign languages than students at top-tier universities such as Peking University and Tsinghua University, because these students feel that their only hope lies in finding work in international trade, tourism, or overseas. Even the privileged classes are not immune to employment difficulties: one child of a high-ranking Xinjiang Uyghur government official graduated from a prestigious mainland university and spent a year searching fruitlessly for work. It was only after securing a personal letter of introduction from Wang Lequan [then Communist Party secretary of Xinjiang] that the young graduate was finally able to secure a job.

2. A unique feature of Xinjiang's natural geography is its desert archipelago of insular, isolated oases. Historically, there has been a vast gap in the amount of government investment given to these different geographical units. This is particularly true of the Uyghur enclaves in Xinjiang's south, where urbanization and industrialization lag far behind the Han Chinese–dominated "Tianshan North Slope Economic Zone." (The Tianshan North Slope Economic Zone, situated at the northern foot of the Tianshan mountain range, is the most economically developed region of Xinjiang. This highly concentrated swath of productive forces forms the developmental core of Xinjiang's modern industry, agriculture, telecommunications, education, science, information technology, and other sectors. Home to over 83 percent of Xinjiang's heavy industry and 62 percent of its light industry, favored with ample

natural resources and robust urban and transportation infrastructure, the zone accounts for over 40 percent of Xinjiang's gross domestic product.) Xinjiang's south is geographically isolated; the Han Chinese cities in the north tend to exclude Uyghurs; and when the surplus rural labor force in the south tries to migrate into the Tianshan North Slope Economic Zone, it is met with restrictions. All these make it even more difficult for southern surplus rural labor to move to urban areas.

3. Severe underinvestment in basic education: there is a vast north–south disparity in educational investment in Xinjiang. Even in southern Xinjiang, one finds stark ethnic inequalities in the allocation of educational resources, particularly in the area of secondary schools. Whether in terms of fiscal investment or number of schools, the proportion of educational resources allocated to Uyghur students is far below what it should be, given their percentage as a proportion of the local population. Moreover, the high school enrollment rate in southern Xinjiang is extremely low, due to the critical lack of investment in basic education: in large Uyghur population centers such as Kuqa County and Shache [Yarkant] County, there is only one high school in each county offering Uyghur-language instruction. As a result, average educational levels in Uyghur communities in southern Xinjiang are extremely low, causing workers to be inadequately equipped for careers in modern agriculture or industry. The surplus rural labor supply spills into the cities, where migrants face severely limited job prospects, forcing them further afield into the interior to look for better opportunities.

4. Since the ethnic unrest of July 2009, nearly all of Xinjiang's Uyghur enclaves have been subject to the constant pressure of "stability maintenance" policies. Rural migrants to the northern city of Urumqi have been expelled in large numbers and forced to return to their villages in the south.

At the same time, local governments have adopted stringent limits on outward population migration, thus exacerbating the problem of rural employment.

Thoughts and Recommendations

The Uyghur unemployment problem is the cumulative result of numerous long-term forces. As such, resolving the dilemma will require a broad-based approach and systematic long-term planning; it will not happen overnight. Simply pouring money from central government coffers into Xinjiang to create a slew of make-work jobs is not the right approach: not only would this prove an undue fiscal burden for the government, it would also transform the Uyghur population into a people dependent upon handouts, engendering a sense of shame and inferiority.

I have the following thoughts on how the issue of unemployment should be addressed systematically:

1. Article 23 of the Regional Ethnic Autonomy Law of the People's Republic of China expressly stipulates that ethnic minorities be given priority in hiring by government institutions and state-owned enterprises.[2] Even taking into consideration the practical difficulties of immediately implementing such a policy, steps should be taken to gradually expand Uyghur employment opportunities and to phase in quotas for the hiring of ethnic minorities in the civil service and state-owned enterprises. At present, public services in Xinjiang suffer from a serious dearth of Uyghur and other ethnic minority employees. Hospitals, post offices, banks, insurance companies, notaries, courts, municipal bureaus and other social service organizations

---

2 The English text of Article 23 of the Regional Ethnic Autonomy Law of the People's Republic of China reads: "When recruiting personnel in accordance with state regulations, enterprises and institutions in ethnic autonomous areas give priority to minority nationalities and may enlist them from the population of minority nationalities in rural and pastoral areas."—Editors

are staffed mainly by Han Chinese who cannot speak Uyghur, causing tremendous inconvenience to Uyghur citizens in their daily lives.

2. The government should take an active role in promoting internal population migration in Xinjiang as a means of alleviating unemployment in the south and preventing further damage to the fragile southern ecosystem. For example, it could oversee a controlled and systematic transfer of a certain proportion of southern Xinjiang's population to the northern industrial belt, or to farms managed by the Xinjiang Production and Construction Corps (XPCC). Instead of spending vast sums of labor and capital to organize rural migrant workers to culturally unfamiliar coastal cities thousands of kilometers away, the regional government should encourage rural-to-urban population shifts within Xinjiang's borders. The Xinjiang Production and Construction Corps, currently suffering from severe manpower shortages due to population drain, has tried all manner of methods to attract labor from other areas of mainland China, but it has done nothing to absorb the surplus rural labor force that exists in southern Xinjiang.

By taking an active role in organizing and guiding population shifts within Xinjiang, the government can alleviate unemployment in the south while also reducing ethnic segregation and helping to dispel the notion, prevalent within the Uyghur community, that the XPCC and the northern cities are being used by Han Chinese to deal with the Uyghur population.

3. Provide more assistance to ethnic minority entrepreneurs. This is the most fundamental, long-term solution to Xinjiang's unemployment problem, and it relies on market-based mechanisms rather than governmental supervision. Since Secretary Zhang Chunxian assumed office, there has been a noticeable improvement in Xinjiang's level of

assistance to ethnic minority entrepreneurs. I recommend broadening this approach to establish a long-term plan aimed at improving the modern management skills of ethnic minority entrepreneurs via exchanges with highly developed coastal regions and prestigious mainland Chinese universities, thus creating a long-term mechanism for the systematic training of minority entrepreneurs. Furthermore, we should foster closer cooperation between Han Chinese and ethnic minority entrepreneurs, encouraging them to bond together in their mutual interest. Having the government train and support a large contingent of minority entrepreneurs is the most convenient way to promote ethnic unity and harmony in Xinjiang.

One detail worth noting: the practice of prominently featuring minority entrepreneurs as speakers at government-organized ethnic unity rallies may not have the desired propaganda effect. Minority entrepreneurs should not be leveraged for government publicity: they have a far more important and effective role to play off the political stage.

4. Increase investment in basic education in minority-populated areas. The government has many long years of unfulfilled promises in this regard, but expanding access to basic education will transform minority peoples' ability to adapt to industrialization and urbanization. In a mere five to ten years, we will begin to see a marked improvement. At the very least, better access to education will significantly reduce the barriers that ethnic minority migrants face when trying to enter the urban labor force. Now that the government has substantially increased investment in basic education in southern Xinjiang, there remain two problems that need to be addressed: countering the preconception that education is useless, and correcting misapprehensions and assuaging people's fears about bilingual education.

5. Establish systematic professional and technical training for ethnic minority workers. Xinjiang suffers from a serious

lack of ethnic minority professional and technical personnel, which makes it difficult for ethnic minorities to enter the technical and industrial workforce. Entrepreneurial skill to start businesses is also in short supply. I propose increasing training for early-career and mid-career specialists in fields suited to the unique economy of the Xinjiang Autonomous Region, in which resource-oriented and state-owned enterprises predominate. For example, the government could work with vocational and technical schools to increase employment opportunities for ethnic minorities in the mining, textile, and agricultural-processing sectors. In fact, work on this has already begun, to positive feedback from Xinjiang's Uyghur community.

I also recommend that the Xinjiang Autonomous Region cooperate with localities in China's more economically developed coastal regions to systematically train up a cohort of technically proficient ethnic minority youth who will form Xinjiang's future technological and entrepreneurial talent pool.

6. Establish brigades of ethnic minority industrial workers. Industrial workers are an essential component and driving force of industrial and economic development. They play a fundamental role in accelerating industrial transformation, promoting technological innovation, improving corporate competitiveness, and so on. Employers in Xinjiang are currently in need of a large number of industrial workers, but they face widespread difficulties in recruiting qualified personnel.

Training up and establishing brigades of ethnic minority industrial workers will help to expand employment opportunities and widen career horizons for minority university and polytechnic graduates. This in turn will increase the employment rate among ethnic minorities and help facilitate their adjustment to modern industrial society.

7. Leverage local and regional advantages to support the development of Xinjiang's own cultural and creative industries. This would both raise employment and allow Xinjiang's cultural influence to radiate across the Central Asian region. Targeted training and practical support would help creative entrepreneurs and small- and medium-size enterprises to expand into the broader Central Asian market. China's information technology, animation, advertising, and other creative sectors enjoy a distinct advantage in the Central Asia market region, but Han Chinese enterprises attempting to enter this market face tremendous cultural and linguistic barriers, whereas Uyghur enterprises possess a natural advantage. By leveraging the technological strength of China's other regions, it is entirely possible for Xinjiang to cultivate local cultural and creative industries with a strong competitive edge in Central Asia. This would allow Xinjiang's ethnic minority populations to transform themselves from cultural importers to cultural exporters, an achievement of immeasurable importance.

II. Bilingual Education

Overview

Besides unemployment, the issue that provokes the most intense reaction within Xinjiang's Uyghur community is the issue of bilingual education. In practice, "bilingual education" in Xinjiang has essentially become "monolingual education" (that is, Mandarin-only education). Within the Uyghur community, there is a widespread belief that the government intends to establish an educational system based on written Chinese and rooted in the idea of "one language, one origin." Suspicions abound that the government is using administrative means to eliminate Uyghur culture and accelerate ethnic and cultural assimilation. With the mandatory implementation of so-called bilingual education, the Uyghur language has become steadily marginalized, not only in the field of education but also in government administration, the judiciary, and other areas. Despite being one of the official languages of the Xinjiang Uyghur Autonomous Region, the Uyghur language has long been deprived of the respect, attention, status, and legal safeguards it deserves.

In practice, the greatest problem with bilingual education in Xinjiang is that it produces a large number of students who are proficient in neither their mother tongues nor in Mandarin. This has led to declining educational standards and difficulties for ethnic minority students, who dread attending school, to master subjects. The bilingual education system in Xinjiang mandates that physics, chemistry, biology, mathematics, and other subjects be taught in Mandarin Chinese, which means that Uyghur and other ethnic minority students are often unable to understand what they are being taught. This policy is responsible, to a large extent, for the steady increase in dropout rates for Uyghur and other ethnic minority students. Another consequence is that many experienced Uyghur primary school teachers have been forced into early retirement or made to leave their faculty positions for jobs unrelated to teaching. Thus, a large number of Uyghur schoolteachers have become direct casualties of government policy on bilingual education.

Bilingual education in Xinjiang has thus increasingly given way to monolingual education, raising grave concerns and causing serious repercussions. This has the potential to spark a larger-scale Uyghur rights movement aimed at defending Uyghur-language education and preventing the elimination of local language and culture. In recent years, Uyghur fears of cultural and linguistic annihilation have been greatly exacerbated by a sharp contraction in Xinjiang's local-language publishing and cultural industries.

This sudden dwindling of Xinjiang's Uyghur-language publishing and cultural industries has profound and far-reaching consequences. Not only does it threaten the demise of Uyghur culture and the suppression of Uyghur intellectuals, it has also caused large sections of the Uyghur community, most of whom live in isolated rural areas, to become completely cut off from contemporary civilization. Southern Xinjiang, taken as a whole, is extremely backward: it is a geographical backwater of scattered, insular oases, and the vast majority of its Uyghur inhabitants do not understand Chinese. For these reasons, the majority of households in southern Xinjiang are cut off from books, newspapers, radio broadcasts, and television programs offering up-to-date information or news about the outside world.

This severing of communication channels means that, notwithstanding a small number of Uyghur elites fluent in Chinese, most traditional Uyghur communities are utterly deprived of access to contemporary news and information. In an increasingly competitive and open social environment, this makes Xinjiang's traditional Uyghur communities inherently less open to external influences than traditional Han Chinese communities in other areas of China. When people are unable to attain the knowledge essential in a modern society, unable to cultivate strength of character for modern life, and cannot acquire healthy modern societal values such as rationality, tolerance, and open-mindedness, they may find themselves in crisis, consumed by fear that they are being increasingly abandoned by modern society. The rapid disintegration of traditional society and the challenges of adapting to a new environment can leave people mired in ignorance, parochialism, savagery, and despair.

Over the past ten years or so, traditional Uyghur society has experienced an unprecedented surge in crime rates, the rapid disintegration of morals, and the spread of religious extremism and cultural conservatism. Add relative impoverishment and an increasing hatred of Han Chinese, and you have a vicious circle that intensifies day by day. It is this, combined with misguided government ethnic policies, that has allowed backward, ignorant, parochial, extremist, isolationist, and fanatical ideologies to proliferate, creating a breeding ground for "the three forces" [of separatism, religious extremism, and terrorism].

Measures such as preaching national unity, making minorities reliant on government handouts, and accelerating the Sinification of China's Uyghur communities are not a sufficient bulwark against separatism, religious extremism, and terrorism. Contrary to the common perception of Uyghur cultural, educational, and publishing industries as being too prone to strengthen Uyghur ethnic and cultural awareness, it is only by allowing these industries to develop and thrive, to keep pace with the times and with history, that we can weaken "the three forces" by denying them ground in which to take root. This is the only feasible long-term method by which to defeat them.

Therefore, we may say that the backwardness of Uyghur cultural, educational, and publishing industries is not only the enemy of Uyghur society, but also the enemy of Han Chinese society.

In fact, nearly all Uyghur families want their children to receive a better-quality education in Mandarin Chinese, and they feel that genuine bilingual education has come too late. Yet at the same time, the prevailing view and mainstream opinion in Uyghur communities is that "bilingual education should not come at the expense of one's mother tongue." Mandarin's special status as China's lingua franca should not be used as an excuse for linguistic discrimination or forced linguistic assimilation. In a nation of diverse ethnicities, shared cultural values should be expressed in diverse ways, not subject to standardization or unification. Education should not be made the "executioner" of native languages and scripts.

As for why bilingual education in Xinjiang has devolved into monolingual education, the answer lies in the slapdash way in which bilingual education policy has been implemented:

1. Deficiencies in technical and basic preparations (finding qualified faculty, investing in school and facilities construction); inadequate consideration of regional differences and

local needs; implementing educational policy in a "one size fits all" fashion.

2. Academic content and curricula that do not take into account either the specific academic needs of ethnic Uyghur students, or the successful experiences of schools in China's other ethnic regions.

3. Xinjiang's limited allotment of teaching staff, poor infrastructure, and low student academic abilities were scarcely sufficient for a monolingual education program, much less a full-scale bilingual education program.

4. Implementing "bilingual education" has actually exacerbated the educational funding gap between Han Chinese and Uyghur students. For example, in the city of Atushi [also spelled Atush or Artux], the Han Chinese population numbers 22,725, the Uyghur population 198,217, and the Kyrgyz population 29,186. If we do not count the Municipal No. 2 School, located forty kilometers outside of the city, Atushi has only three high schools: one Chinese-language school (Prefectural No. 2 High School) and two Uyghur-language schools (Prefectural No. 1 High School and Municipal No. 2 High School). Class sizes in the Uyghur schools average more than fifty students per classroom, whereas the Chinese school averages only thirty students per class. Differences in teaching quality and levels of educational investment have widened the educational gap between Han Chinese and Uyghur students, both in terms of their access to knowledge and their ability to master new subject matter.

Thoughts and Recommendations

1. Xinjiang needs true bilingual education. The [Korean-language] bilingual education program in Yanbian Autonomous Prefecture is a typical success story. Xinjiang can draw from that experience in restructuring its own bilingual educational content and curriculum.

2. In ethnic-minority populated areas, increase investment in the hardware and software required to provide true bilingual education, and redress the grievous imbalance in educational resources allocated to different ethnic groups.

3. Train qualified teachers. Currently, the biggest impediment to bilingual education is a serious shortage of qualified teachers. It will be difficult to alter this situation in the short term, but by focusing on systematic training of existing teachers, we can gradually reduce or dispel the regional disparities among teachers of bilingual education.

4. Exam-based university selection of minority students: although the current system of adding points to the university entrance-exam scores of ethnic minority test-takers is in line with the central government policy of favoring minority candidates, in practice, many of the true beneficiaries of this preferential scoring system are academically accomplished minority students who do not require preferential treatment, or even affluent, well-connected Han Chinese students. It might be possible to replace the "added points" section of the exam with test matter related to Xinjiang's ethnic and cultural diversity. Not only would this signal to Uyghur students that Xinjiang's multiethnic and multicultural traditions have not been forgotten by the educational system, it would also deepen everyone's understanding of Xinjiang's ethnic and cultural diversity, thus shaping a richer and more inclusive national identity and consciousness.

5. Raise the number and prestige of ethnic minority cultural and publishing endeavors in order to reverse the rapid decline of minority cultural industries. In terms of fiscal policy, increase government investment and support for ethnic minority cultural, educational, and publishing industries, and accelerate Uyghur-language participation and access to modern information technology. Both the regional and the central government should advance

Uyghur rural society by promoting knowledge of modern social life and modern production methods and making this a key element in long-term planning.

With regard to Uyghur folk culture, the government of the Xinjiang Autonomous Region should search for ways to encourage and support grassroots cultural initiatives in this field. The regional government should also begin experimenting with gradual reforms of the ethnic minority cultural and educational publishing industries: for example, introducing market-based mechanisms or objective quality targets, harnessing the initiative and enthusiasm of existing staff, and avoiding the current problem of overstaffing.

6. Increase regional or national government support for specialized research and scholarship on the social transformations affecting Uyghur communities. Encourage the participation of mainland Chinese and even overseas scholars and academics, so that China's rulers can draw on their collective wisdom and counsel to resolve the nation's ethnic and social dilemmas. In mainland China at the moment, there is an almost complete dearth of worthwhile academic research on this topic. One hopes that if scholars are allowed more academic independence, it will help to fill this void.

7. Establish a plan and systematic targets for training a new breed of top-tier ethnic minority intellectuals and incorporate them into national planning via funding for specially earmarked projects.

Xinjiang suffers from a dearth of ethnic minority intellectuals, at least those who meet the strict modern criteria for intellectuals. Moribund educational and research institutions and outmoded systems of personnel training and advancement have deprived Xinjiang of a true community of ethnic minority intellectuals. Whether the task is promoting social progress in Xinjiang, improving the lives of ethnic minorities, or advancing national identity and cohesion among minority elites, a highly qualified community of ethnic minority intellectuals is essential to the task. Allowing more ethnic minority intellectuals to enter the mainstream confers honor upon them and their communities, and that honor serves to strengthen their sense of national identity and cohesion.

III. Religion

Overview

Since the July 2009 ethnic unrest in Xinjiang, religious fervor within China's Uyghur community has been rising steadily. Whether in traditional villages in southern Xinjiang, among urban officials and intellectuals, or even on college campuses in Beijing, there has been a quiet upsurge in religious conservatism—and the percentage of youthful conservative adherents is at an all-time high. Some observers have noted that during religious services at mosques it is not uncommon to see young people praying silently, with tears streaming down their faces. This is a social signal worthy of our close attention.

As an overt symbol of a people's cultural and ethnic identity, religion comes second only to language; in the most extreme circumstances, religion can become the final spiritual refuge for a people.

The two most serious aspects of the religious problem in Xinjiang are as follows:

1. First is the enormous backlash generated by strict government controls on religion. Xinjiang's south is home to approximately 24,000 mosques, and each mosque has a designated religious leader supported by the government: one cadre per mosque, responsible for denying admittance to outsiders, youths, or regular worshippers beyond the allotted quota. Such stringent controls display utter

disregard for the feelings of believers, consume vast amounts of manpower and resources, and arouse great discontent among the citizenry.

2. Second is the proliferation of underground religious activities, in marked contrast to the government's failed religious policies of recent years. Ultra-conservative and xenophobic strains of religious thought imported from Afghanistan, Pakistan, and other places are spreading rapidly in Xinjiang, and are being disseminated via the religious underground. Increasing numbers of extremely conservatively dressed citizens attest to the popularity of this religious trend. In private, some Uyghur intellectuals decry the new conservatism, complaining that Uyghurs no longer dress like Uyghurs, but like Arabs.

Although Xinjiang has no shortage of Kazakh- and Chinese-language versions of the Koran, Uyghur-language versions of the Koran are not available for sale on the open market. This distinction could easily incline people to suspect that restrictive government religious policies are being targeted at a specific ethnic group. Some years ago, the Saudi king sent one million free copies of the Koran to Xinjiang, where they circulated freely among the local populace. After incidents of ethnic unrest in 1996 and 1997, these copies of the Koran were recalled; these days, a pirated copy of the Koran sells for between 50 and 80 Chinese yuan on the underground market.

Most Uyghur intellectuals are wary of and opposed to extremist religious ideology. They recognize the contributions of Communist Party atheism and secular education in abolishing superstition, fanaticism, and ignorance within the Uyghur community. And yet the government's current draconian religious policies in Xinjiang are repugnant to Uyghur intellectuals, even to those most repelled by religious fanaticism.

Causes

Although the Chinese government is now much more tolerant of religious enthusiasm than it has been in the past, its long-standing adherence to atheism and lack of systematic research on religious issues mean that, when confronted with issues involving religion, the government tends to find itself on the defensive.

Specifically, when it comes to dealing with religious issues in Xinjiang, official disdain for the special status of religion in ethnic minority communities makes it hard to see where government promotion of secularization ends and the suppression of ethnic minority culture begins. Particularly with regard to Islam, the government tends to oscillate wildly between confidence and fear—confidence inspired by the machinery of the one-party state, and fear fueled by a basic lack of religious knowledge.

Since 1997, opposing "the three forces" has been the paramount task of local government. Along the way, however, the policy of opposing religious extremism has morphed into a policy of opposing religious tradition and suppressing normal expressions of religious belief.

Recently, Xinjiang's government has launched a vigorous propaganda push on the dangers of religious extremism, and it is on high alert against religious extremism and its effects. Extremist religious ideology is certainly unacceptable: even from an Islamic perspective, it is a distortion of traditional religious thought. But government policy in practice all too often veers toward rigid uniformity: indiscriminately lumping the wearing of headscarves, veils, or beards into the same category as religious extremism, for example, or banning men with beards and women with veils or headscarves from entering buildings or public places. These and other persistent infringements on Uyghur human rights are, to a large extent, responsible for creating antagonism between Uyghurs and the government, thus amplifying Han–Uyghur tensions.

While there is no denying that Xinjiang does indeed have a problem with religious extremism, it needs to be emphasized that extremist religious ideology has never dominated the mainstream in Uyghur society, and its actual influence within the Uyghur community is quite limited. More important, traditional Uyghur culture has always displayed a marked resistance to extremist religious ideology. At present, the threat posed by religious extremism appears to be greatly exaggerated, both in government propaganda and in the public imagination. Enacting inappropriate control measures based on this flawed understanding will, objectively speaking, only drive people to embrace more extremist religious views. Moreover, when it comes to voicing criticism of extremist religious ideology, this criticism should come primarily from esteemed and learned leaders within the religious community, rather than from secular intellectuals speaking on matters outside their purview. And the minute details of citizens' sartorial habits—clothes, beards, scarves, and the like—should never be singled out for criticism.

In order to understand the problem of religious extremism in the Uyghur community, we must recognize the following key points: (1) It is of great importance to clearly define what is extremist religious ideology and extremist religious behavior; (2) The goal of opposing extremist religious ideology should be to protect and safeguard normal, everyday religious activity; (3) Within Uyghur society, religion was originally closely tied to cultural customs and traditions, but now religion has been stripped of its status and deprived of its traditional authority figures; (4) Uyghur society has lost its mechanisms for moral grounding and cultural adjustment; (5) There are no normal channels for positive voices to make themselves heard; and (6) In order to protect their posts and their perks of office, some officials are more than willing to burn the wheat along with the chaff.

Currently, Xinjiang's coercive stability-maintenance policies, particularly in the area of religion, are having a grave impact on the lives, jobs, and mobility of Xinjiang's Uyghur population. If the government does not change its thinking and tactics with respect to religious issues, I fear that religion will become the single biggest cause of ethnic strife and social discord in Xinjiang.

Thoughts and Recommendations

The entire Islamic world, in fact, is being confronted with religious problems along the path to modernity. Turkey, Malaysia, the United Arab Emirates, Egypt, and other countries have found different and successful ways to balance religion and modernity. There is no shame in learning from their successes or adopting their methods of dealing with religion, in much the same way that China, in the early days of economic reform and opening, looked to the West for experience and guidance.

1. Establish institutional arrangements for the management of religious sites and places of worship. Places of worship offer a natural way for communities to bond, and the government can draw on foreign experience to develop standards governing the physical size, congregation size, social organization, etc. of places of worship. To facilitate the ability of citizens to practice their faith, the government should allow one place of worship to be built within each defined area or range. Each place of worship should also be equipped with clergy who have been officially recognized and certified by the government, in accordance with clear-cut rules and regulations. This will help to avert the proliferation of home-based and underground places of worship that have sprung up in response to draconian restrictions on the ordinary religious needs of citizens. In establishing such a system, it would not hurt to publicize the fact that some elements of the system were adopted from abroad (from a secular country such as Turkey, for example) in order to defuse opposition.

2. Establish a system of religious training and certification for clergy members. There are some religious professionals who, despite their lack of certification or authority, still

ESSAY

manage to attract adherents who believe them to possess religious wisdom. Professional clergy must complete systematic training and earn some official certification (for example, from the Islamic Association of China). In addition to systematic training in religious knowledge and scholarship, clergy should also possess some knowledge of the modern social sciences, to nurture a mindset that is open, progressive, and attuned to the needs of modern society. In particular, studying how religion and modern society interact and adapt in other countries and learning from their experiences will help provide clergy with a broader and more open-minded perspective.

Regarding the vocational and educational training of clergy, a long-range, well-organized system of religious training should be established in collaboration with top-tier institutions of religious learning in Xinjiang, nationwide, and even overseas, in order to gradually train a core group of erudite and broad-minded clergy. In addition, allowing local institutions of religious learning such as the Xinjiang Islamic Institute to strengthen communication and ties with other institutions of religious learning at home and abroad will bolster the quality of local religious scholarship.

3. To satisfy public demand for religious texts, allow the legal importation and publication of overseas editions of contemporary religious texts. Uyghur-language versions of religious texts are nearly impossible to find in Xinjiang today; the copies that do circulate underground are generally smuggled in from Afghanistan, Pakistan, or Saudi Arabia. But in fact, Turkey, Malaysia, and other successful secular Islamic nations have long been compiling and codifying contemporary editions of religious texts that have not only met the religious needs of their citizens, but also helped to usher in more open and modern societal values. If the government were to organize the translation and publication of these religious texts from abroad, it

would satisfy the religious needs of the local community, impede the underground market for extremist religious publications, and promote the spread of moderate, open, and inclusive religious values.

4. Improve research and investment in religion. China is a country with a large Muslim population, but Chinese religious scholarship that meets modern academic standards of quality, particularly scholarship pertaining to Islam, is virtually nonexistent. China should have prestigious Islamic Institutes, as well as other respected institutions dedicated to the study of Islam. The government should also encourage non-Muslim scholars to participate in religious research and scholarship that satisfies the needs of religious believers and religious scholarship and meets the demands of social development and transformation. Lastly, increasing research and investment in religion will serve to amplify China's voice in the Islamic world and allow it to play a more active role.

5. Leverage the influence of religion in traditional society to positive effect. For communities steeped in religious tradition, the clergy are an irreplaceable and profoundly influential component of society. Particularly in the comparatively insular, economically underdeveloped, and culturally conservative rural communities of southern Xinjiang, the best ways to disseminate modern ideas and information are via the market and via religion.

   Indeed, religious leaders have also been thinking about how to address the issue of social transformation. The government has nothing to lose by creating the conditions and opportunities for the clergy to join in this effort, allowing them to contribute their experience, intelligence, wisdom, and considerable social influence. Religious leaders and ordinary citizens alike do not want to see a society plagued by unrest, chaos, or hatred. Religion is the pursuit of virtue, after all, and religious leaders are cautious and conservative by nature. Instead of their voices being suppressed, they should be allowed to take their rightful place in the public discourse, so that they may use their own language to offer comfort and consolation to their community.

6. Make policy regarding the Hajj [the Muslim pilgrimage to Mecca] more transparent and open. It would be fair to call the Hajj policy one of the greatest failures of religious policy in Xinjiang. Simply put, the Hajj is something that all devout Muslims aspire to; completing the pilgrimage to Mecca imbues a person with a certain amount of social prestige upon their return, but it does not cause them to become extremist or fanatical. At present, there are stringent bureaucratic criteria for being allowed to go on the Hajj, but this bureaucratic process need not be so opaque. Every year, Saudi Arabia issues quotas for the number of pilgrims allowed from each country. In Xinjiang, only a lucky few meet the qualifications. The quota process could certainly be carried out in a much more open and transparent manner—for example, by publicizing China's quota and explaining how this quota is allocated. As it stands, the quota system has bred serious bureaucratic corruption and has aroused intense feelings in ethnic minority communities.

IV. Ethnic Alienation and Segregation

Overview

Among the openly talked-about problems affecting ethnic relations in Xinjiang, perhaps the most important is the increasing sense of alienation among ethnic minorities. But beyond this psychological sense of alienation, there is another, even more severe problem that few people (Uyghurs in particular) are willing to discuss openly: the problem of physical ethnic segregation.

By physical or macro-level segregation, I mean that Xinjiang's Han Chinese population tends to be clustered in areas of relatively high population density. In fact, the vast majority of Xinjiang's Han Chinese population is concentrated in three areas, all of which are effectively off-limits to Uyghurs: Xinjiang Production and Construction Corps (XPCC) areas; Xinjiang's capital city of Urumqi; and cities such as Shihezi and Kuitun that are located in the Tianshan North Slope Economic Zone.

As for micro-level segregation, cities such as Urumqi with mixed ethnic populations (of Han Chinese, Uyghur, and other minorities) tend to be heavily balkanized, divided into distinct ethnic enclaves. This is particularly true since the ethnic unrest of July 2009: statistics on Urumqi, Xinjiang's largest ethnically mixed city, in the most recent issue of the Xinjiang Statistical Yearbook, published in 2010, reveal an increased tendency among both Han Chinese and Uyghur residents to leave mixed neighborhoods and relocate to neighborhoods dominated by their own ethnic group.

This conscious decision to "leave the ethnic enclaves of others" is unlike other forms of ethnic discrimination or animosity (for example, taxi drivers refusing passengers of another ethnic group) that can be easily identified and halted. The historical impact of this decision will be enormous and far-reaching, because if the daily lives of Han Chinese and Uyghurs become separate, it will exacerbate mutual feelings of estrangement and alienation. To some extent, this is a subtle form of "Palestinization."

The flip side of ethnic segregation in Xinjiang is status segregation. Nearly all Han Chinese in Xinjiang live in urban areas or "within the system" [of government entities or government-controlled entities], while the vast majority of Uyghurs live in rural areas or "outside the system." The two-tiered system that manifests itself in other areas of China as a divide between rural and urban manifests itself in Xinjiang as a divide between Han Chinese and Uyghur. It goes without saying that this sort of ethnic segregation has a profound impact on the Uyghur sense of ethnic and national identity. In fact, it calls to mind similar systems of segregation in Palestine and South Africa. Uyghurs in China are "noncitizens" or "second-class citizens," and XPCC outposts are widely regarded as the equivalent of Jewish settlements in the Gaza Strip. This status segregation has caused more than a few Uyghur intellectuals to liken Han Chinese to white Afrikaners and Uyghurs to South African Blacks.

The skewed ethnic population distribution in Xinjiang has created a subconscious dichotomy in the minds of Han Chinese people between "their part of Xinjiang" (that is, the Uyghur-populated south) and "our part of Xinjiang" (the Han Chinese–populated north). In truth, there is no concept of Xinjiang as unified community or polity.

Causes

The ethnic population distribution pattern in Xinjiang today is largely the product of historical and systemic causes.

After Liberation [the establishment of the People's Republic of China in 1949], the central government mobilized a large-scale effort to promote migration to Xinjiang. In line with the political climate of the time, nearly all of the Han Chinese migrants to Xinjiang were state employees, and most were assigned to the Xinjiang Production and Construction Corps (XPCC). Furthermore, central-government industrial investment and systemic planning in Xinjiang was designed to complement the aforementioned migration program.

In recent decades, Xinjiang's urbanization and development have been concentrated in the north, with the bulk of development projects and support going to a few primarily Han Chinese northern enclaves, while Uyghur enclaves in southern Xinjiang have received almost no material support for urban development. Meanwhile, the XPCC's ever-expanding urbanization has pushed beyond the big cities of Shihezi and Kuitun to create a new group of cities such as Fukang, Wujiaqu, Tiemenguan, and Beitun, controlled by the XPCC and populated mainly by Han Chinese. Between 2011 and 2015, the period covering China's Twelfth Five-Year Plan, the XPCC will accelerate construction on a number of cities: Wuxing (XPCC Fifth Division), Kokdala (XPCC Fourth Division), Huyanghe (XPCC Seventh Division), Hongxing (XPCC Thirteenth Division), and Yulong (XPCC Fourteenth Division). These XPCC cities have long excluded Uyghurs and other ethnic minorities, thus further marginalizing these groups.

These systematic factors are tantamount to furthering the physical segregation of Han Chinese and Uyghurs, intensifying the sense of unfairness and "noncitizenship" felt by the Uyghur community, and reducing opportunities for Xinjiang's different ethnic groups to interact with one another in their daily lives. By pushing expansion and urbanization, the XPCC is tearing Xinjiang apart, worsening an already serious state of ethnic apartheid. In contrast with the XPCC approach, urban expansion in Shache County, Moyu County, Jiashi County, and other areas of the south would be much more beneficial in reducing the disparities between north and south and allowing all ethnic groups a fair share of the fruits of development.[3]

Thoughts and Recommendations

The Hakka, Teochew, and other ethnic groups of China's southeastern seaboard had a long history of clan warfare and centuries-old feuds—that is, until the advent of modern industry and commerce created deeper linkages between profits and the social division of labor, thus helping to bring about rapid social integration and dispel ancient enmities. In the long run, prospects for Xinjiang's ethnic relations may be similarly optimistic, but

---

3 There are numerous alternate spellings for these counties. Shache County is also known as Yarkant or Yarkand; Moyu County as Karakax or Qaraqash; and Jiashi County as Payzawat or Peyziwat.—Editors

there is one important prerequisite: we must reduce or eliminate the physical separation between ethnic groups, rather than allow segregation to continue unabated.

In fact, in all multiethnic nations, the process of dismantling or destroying barriers of segregation is an important barometer of, and a means to achieving, peaceful ethnic relations.

1. Stop building mono-ethnic cities. Xinjiang's urbanization efforts are now targeted at building up a number of key areas: if development in these areas proceeds according to current targets and plans, it will create an even greater number of mono-ethnic cities. When we are building new cities and towns, I suggest transferring a certain amount of population from the south, insofar as circumstances allow. Use the hand of government to guide population movements in the region and promote the formation of new, ethnically mixed cities. The government could also allow some flexibility in the use of financial resources to improve the ethnic balance of areas and operations within its purview.

2. Clannishness is part of human nature, but when it comes to allocating government resources, we should dedicate those resources to creating diverse and integrated communities. Singapore is an excellent case in point. As a multiethnic and multicultural rising city-state, Singapore has used its system of public housing to increase mutual understanding among different ethnic groups and promote a more tolerant, open, and pluralistic society. By deliberately bringing people of different ethnicities and cultures to live together in proportions that parallel the overall ethnic population distribution, Singapore has leveraged government resources to build an ethnically integrated and mutually inclusive society.

   In ethnically mixed cities such as Urumqi, the government could provide low-rent, subsidized, or public housing in such a way as to encourage the formation of ethnically mixed communities and to avoid creating mono-ethnic urban enclaves. In addition, when hiring or assigning work to cadres, civil servants, state-owned enterprises or other entities under government control, the government should do its utmost to facilitate interaction and communication between different ethnic communities. This could include assigning Uyghur cadres to work in mainly Han Chinese neighborhoods, and Han Chinese cadres to work in mainly Uyghur neighborhoods, and doing everything possible to maximize opportunities for integration and daily contact between the two ethnicities.

3. Employees of government bureaus and public service industries such as banking, transportation, utilities, and insurance should be required to acquire, over time, a certain degree of fluency in local languages. If employees of these institutions can display a certain mastery of languages other than Mandarin, it will help convince ethnic minorities that the government is not merely a government for the Han Chinese, but a government dedicated to serving the needs of all of its citizens, regardless of ethnicity. It would also, in the minds of Han Chinese employees, help to reinforce the impression of Xinjiang as a multiethnic and multicultural autonomous region, markedly different from other regions of China populated solely by Han Chinese.

V. Distrust of Ethnic Minority Officials and Intellectuals

Overview

Widespread official distrust of ethnic minority cadres and intellectuals is one blatantly obvious and tremendously important facet of Xinjiang's ethnic problem. In 1997, the Chinese Communist Party Central Committee's "Document No. 7" marked a watershed moment in Xinjiang's ethnic conflict: in it, the Party Central Committee expressed its belief that the biggest problem facing Xinjiang was the threat of the "three forces" [of terrorism, religious extremism, and separatism]. In Xinjiang, this new policy thrust resulted in a series of measures that soon transformed the entire Uyghur population into suspected separatists and precipitated a rapid decline in the status of Uyghur cadres and the responsibilities given to them. This marginalization of Uyghur cadres in turn bred a subtle climate of distrust between Han and Uyghur officials as they went about their duties.

Although today's Chinese Communist Party is a political party that transcends ethnic, class, and interest group boundaries, the consensus within Uyghur society can be summed up as follows: Han Chinese equal power, therefore power equals Han Chinese; Han Chinese equal the Communist Party, therefore the Communist Party equals Han Chinese.

Uyghur officials account for a very small proportion of total government officials, and Uyghurs who occupy positions of real power—bureau-level cadres or higher—are even rarer. Some powerful governmental departments such as Finance, Public Security, and the SASAC [State-Owned Assets Supervision and Administration Commission] have virtually no Uyghur officials. The situation is even more glaring in Xinjiang's state-owned enterprises: one would be hard-pressed to cite even a single example of a state-owned enterprise headed by a Uyghur.

Whether in the Chinese People's Political Consultative Conference [CPPCC], the National People's Congress [NPC], or the Communist Party Congress, the number of Uyghur committee members and representatives is disproportionately low. Underrepresentation and low levels of political participation reflect the declining political status and increasing marginalization of Uyghurs in China.

The CPPCC, entrusted with the role of "political participation and deliberation," is an important component of the Chinese political system, but the number of ethnic Uyghur CPPCC committee members is disproportionately low, both at the national and the regional level. Among the thirteen chairmen or deputy chairmen of the Xinjiang Uyghur Autonomous Region CPPCC, only four are Uyghur. At the regional level, Uyghur representation in the CPPCC is numerically and proportionally small, and the cadres tend to be low in rank.

In the Twelfth National Committee of the CPPCC, only 10 members [of 2,237] are Uyghur, continuing the downward trend of recent years. And of the 107 members of the Xinjiang CPPCC new Standing Committee, only 27 (about 25 percent) are Uyghur. There is a serious discrepancy between the small number of Uyghur CPPCC committee members and the proportion of Xinjiang's population that is Uyghur (about 47 percent), a discrepancy that is at odds with the rightful stature of the Uyghur people as a self-governing ethnic group within the Xinjiang Uyghur Autonomous Region.

Of the 2,987 delegates who attended the 12th National People's Congress this year, only 409 were ethnic minorities, an average of 1 delegate for every 270,000 ethnic minority citizens. Among the minority delegates, only 25 were Uyghur (23 from the Xinjiang Uyghur Autonomous Region, and 2 from the People's Liberation Army delegation), which works out to 1 delegate for every 400,000 Uyghur citizens. Although the overall proportion of minority delegates exceeded the proportion of ethnic minorities relative to China's total population, the opposite was true for Uyghur delegates, whose numbers were disproportionately low.

As we can see from these numbers, Uyghurs have been excluded from the center of power, and their political stature in China is in sharp decline.

In the early days of the People's Republic of China, the biggest issue facing the Chinese Communist Party was how to train up an echelon of competent and qualified ethnic minority cadres. Now that the Party has been in power for sixty years, however, finding talented minority cadres should not be a problem. There are long-term factors that impact the training of minority cadres, but the distrust of minority cadres derives from a certain historical context. It is widely believed that after 1997, the stature and perceived trustworthiness of minority cadres plummeted. This created a vicious cycle: marginalization bred distrust, which led to anger and alienation, and this alienation was then turned back into an excuse for finding minority cadres untrustworthy.

Political marginalization and the sense that they are not fully trusted can create problems for minority cadres. Compared to their Han Chinese colleagues, ethnic minority cadres tend to become more timid and risk-averse, afraid to voice their opinions, and inclined to grumble in private. A decade of tension has created a situation in which no one within Xinjiang's Uyghur community dares to speak up. As Deng Xiaoping once said: "The silence of the masses is a terrifying thing." But having Uyghur cadres who are afraid to speak up is an even more terrifying thing, because these cadres tend to have a fairly accurate grasp of prevailing moods and attitudes within the Uyghur community. Over time, their silence makes it difficult for local government policy makers to hear the voices of the Uyghur community.

Uyghur intellectuals find themselves in much the same dilemma. Long-running social tensions and a coercive atmosphere have led to a collective silence from the Uyghur intelligentsia, a group that should, by rights, be more outspoken. Even their social contribution and creativity have, unlike in the past, diminished. And their sense of critical awareness and social responsibility is generally weak, especially compared to Han Chinese intellectuals in the interior.

Naturally, nationalism is the business of a nation's elite, and cadres and intellectuals represent a gathering of the national elite. Their ideas can sway the emotions of an entire community, giving expression to the interests of that community, while also serving as the voices of moderation and rationality. When cadres and intellectuals of the Uyghur elite find themselves increasingly constrained by narrower and narrower circumstances, their resentment, depression, and ethnic grievances cannot help but spread through the entire community.

The existence of Uyghur cadres reflects the issue of the political legitimacy of the Xinjiang Uyghur Autonomous Region. If the appointment of Zhang Chunxian fails to restore the trust of Uyghur cadres and intellectuals to pre-1997 levels, then the Uyghur elite will likely lose confidence altogether and perhaps even plunge into despair, for Zhang's appointment has so far given hope to a considerable number of people who have long believed that the present mistrust of Uyghurs is an exception to the rule, the product of stability policies run amok under a few dictatorial leaders, rather than a true reflection of Han Chinese attitudes toward Uyghurs.

Causes

1. Inadequate training of ethnic minority cadres. Selecting and training a cohort of minority cadres was an important component of national ethnic policy during the first few decades of Chinese Communist Party rule. Because of low education rates, lagging social development, and a shortage of qualified candidates in minority areas, the government put a great deal of effort into selecting and training minority cadres who would later help to implement national ethnic policy.

   These days, however, the selection criteria and training methods used for minority cadres seem to have fallen behind the times. Qualities such as competence, vision, and breadth of knowledge should be considered just as important as political reliability. The present system of training does not adequately factor in just how much Xinjiang lags behind other areas of mainland China. Some key postings may simply require higher levels of conceptual skill, knowledge, governing ability, and cognitive capacity.

2. Stability maintenance policies have elevated perfectly normal feelings and expressions of ethnic pride and ethnic

self-interest to the level of secessionism. By constantly emphasizing the dangers of local ethnic nationalism, the government has overlooked growing Han Chinese chauvinism. In Xinjiang, the inverse of local ethnic nationalism is a growing trend toward Han Chinese chauvinism and ethnocentrism.

Thoughts and Recommendations

1. Ethnic sentiment is an innate and natural emotion, but it can also be controlled, guided, and balanced. In the same way that we recognize that different economic classes have different interests and demands, we should also recognize that different ethnic groups have their own specific interests and demands, and we should take this into consideration when balancing the government's interest in national unity with respect for the interests of ethnic minorities. Originally, there was a tacit agreement to respect Uyghur ethnic sentiment, and such unwritten rules and their underlying logic should be clearly spelled out.

2. Overall, there are too few Uyghur cadres, particularly in the upper echelons. We should look to the long run and begin to train a cohort of qualified, top-tier ethnic minority cadres. To enhance Xinjiang's long-term development prospects, we should consider a bold plan to send young ethnic minority cadres from Xinjiang to undergo intensive study and field training in the economically developed regions of China's southeastern seaboard. Training minority cadres in the southeast would not only help spread progressive ideas, it would also fundamentally deepen emotional ties to other areas of China among Xinjiang's minority elites.

3. According to the Regional Ethnic Autonomy Law of the People's Republic of China, Uyghur and Mandarin enjoy equal status as working languages, but at present few Han Chinese cadres speak Uyghur. This is especially true in

southern Xinjiang, where poor language skill among Han Chinese cadres has been widely criticized. The government should encourage local Han Chinese cadres to work harder to attain at least a certain level of proficiency in Uyghur or another minority language, and these language skills should gradually be incorporated into the performance assessments of local party cadres and civil servants. Central government staff would be exempt from this rule.

4. In conjunction with ethnic demographics, pay more attention to the proportional ethnic distribution of cadres. Xinjiang's demographic pattern of small ethnic enclaves will not change overnight, but we should try, as much as possible, to facilitate integration and exchange via staff assignments and transfers. In regions populated mainly by Han Chinese, it might be appropriate to increase the proportion of Uyghur cadres; in Uyghur-populated areas of southern Xinjiang, it might be appropriate to raise the proportion of not only Han Chinese cadres, but also of Kazakh, Mongolian, and other ethnic minority cadres.

5. Cultivate a group of talented Uyghur intellectual elites. At present, Xinjiang has not yet given rise to a true community of modern intellectuals. There is a shortage of Uyghur talent at party- and state-run research institutions, particularly in the social sciences. Systematically cultivating a group of top-tier Uyghur intellectuals will not only help lead traditional Uyghur society into modernity, it will also, over time, imbue the Uyghur elite with a broader national perspective and help inspire confidence in them—this, indeed, might be the greatest contribution of all.

6. Commission research on the topic of social development in Xinjiang. Academic research regarding Xinjiang's social development lags Xinjiang's reality: Xinjiang's particularly closed nature means that local research on the subject is somewhat out of date, in terms of conceptual and theoretical tools. To a certain extent, some of the academic research

being done in Xinjiang today serves little purpose but to endorse existing local policy decisions. The issue of social development in Xinjiang is particularly complex and will require research projects, commissioned at the highest national level, capable of attracting the long-term participation of outstanding intellectuals nationwide. We should also encourage more local intellectuals in Xinjiang, particularly Uyghur intellectuals, to participate in these long-term studies.

VI. The Xinjiang Production and Construction Corps

Overview

Today's Xinjiang Production and Construction Corps [XPCC, or simply "the Corps"] is a most insular and unique organization. It is often informally described as "an army with no military budget; a government that pays taxes; a labor union made up of farmers; and a business that is a society of its own."

Opinion regarding the role and function of the Corps is polarized. Officially and in public, the Corps is portrayed as a protector and symbol of social stability in Xinjiang, as well a symbol of Xinjiang's pioneering spirit. Private opinion is a different matter: privately, a large number of ordinary Corps members complain that the Corps system is the root cause of their growing impoverishment and backwardness. And within the Uyghur community, the Corps stands as a symbol of ethnic antagonism.

A social survey we conducted reveals that Uyghur attitudes to Han Chinese vary depending on the type of Chinese community. For example, Uyghurs felt closest to locally born Han Chinese, and most at odds with Han Chinese Corps members. Uyghur attitudes toward other Han Chinese migrants to Xinjiang fell somewhere in between.

In fact, the vast majority of ordinary Uyghurs have few opportunities to interact with Han Chinese Corps members.

They therefore lack a basic understanding of realities within the Corps, and may even harbor profound misconceptions. For many Uyghurs, their sole impression of the Corps comes through television news footage, which may lead them to believe that everyone in the Corps lives in places like Shihezi: lovely cities with broad avenues, forests of tall buildings, pristine environments, and living standards that far outstrip the rest of Xinjiang. In fact, most people in the Corps live on farms; they work much harder and earn much less than non-Corps Han Chinese living in nearby rural areas. For many years running, the income of Corps members has ranked dead last in the national income rankings. The reality of life in the Corps is that it is insular and increasingly impoverished.

Not coincidentally, Uyghur antipathy for the Corps is the direct result of a constant stream of government propaganda trumpeting the political role and accomplishments of the Corps, particularly its role in opposing "the three forces."

The Xinjiang Production and Construction Corps was initially established to serve three main functions: military, political, and economic. In today's environment, the Corps' military role has all but disappeared, while its political role has been bolstered. The political functions of the Corps can be outlined as follows: (1) maintain social stability and deter separatism; (2) promote ethnic interaction and national unity; (3) effectively manage the continued existence and development of the Corps itself.

Truly, only the first two functions have any value or inherent meaning. Yet judging by the current state of the Corps, those two functions have long since ceased to exist. Various official publications repeatedly cite the same example of the Corps' role in maintaining stability and deterring separatism: quelling a 1990 "counter-revolutionary armed rebellion" in Baren Township, Akto County, in Xinjiang's southwest. In fact, although the nearby Corps militia was called up, it played no substantive role in putting down the rebellion.

If something were to happen in the present situation, it should be the People's Armed Police that responds, rather than the XPCC militia. Taking the unusual step of mobilizing the Corps' civilian militia would be politically inappropriate in the extreme: after all, why should Han Chinese civilians be given the responsibility, or even the right, to used armed force to suppress an uprising among Uyghurs? This would only serve to inflame ethnic tensions. Another fact we must note is that the Corps has almost completely lost its ability to mobilize and mount a rapid armed response in the event of an emergency. This is partly because the Corps does not, at a grassroots level, have control over the movements of its young labor force of fighting age, and partly because the young labor force of the Corps is declining due to manpower drain.

As for using the Corps to promote ethnic interaction and national unity, it is out of the question. In China, combining insular political structures with local communities all too often leads to antagonism and estrangement: witness the estrangement between inland rural communities and China's "Third-Front" factories, or between Beijing's traditional *hutong* neighborhoods and massive Socialist-era government compounds.[4] The XPCC is an insular institution by nature, isolated even from Xinjiang's local Han Chinese community. Far from being a symbol of ethnic interaction and national unity, the Corps has come to be seen by the Uyghur community as a symbol of ethnic segregation, a fact that says a lot about its character.

The current status of the Corps can be summarized as follows: On the political front, not only has the Corps lost its role as a deterrent against separatism, it has lost its political raison d'être.

---

4   The "Third Front" program, carried out between 1964 and 1971, was an attempt to create a secure inland military-industrial base that could serve as a bulwark in the event of China being drawn into a war. The program involved large-scale investment in defense, technology, basic industries, transportation, and infrastructure, and the relocation of factories from vulnerable coastal ("first front") and central ("second front") cities to remote rural regions of southwestern and northwestern China.—Editors

On the fiscal front, the Corps has become a financial burden to the government. On the social front, the Corps is facing a severe population drain. On the economic front, the Corps must contend with an increasingly impoverished constituency. On the legal front, the precise legal standing (or even the legality) of the Corps has never been adequately established. On the ethnic relations front, the Corps has become a symbol of ethnic antagonism. On the institutional front, the Corps is the last bastion of centralized economic planning in China—it has failed to implement even the "contract responsibility system," a system of market-based economic reforms that have been in place in other areas of China for over three decades. On the status front, the Corps is an awkward amalgam of "party, military, government and private industry": it is all of the above, and yet none of the above. Finally, on the local relations front, the Corps has never served its stated purpose of "clarifying and coordinating" relations with the local population.

Causes

The XPCC is essentially a modern version of the ancient *biantun* system [of agriculturally self-supporting military garrisons]. It is the outgrowth of a particular system during a particular period of history. More than any other organizational system, the Corps is an embodiment of China's six decades of centralized economic planning. That it continues to exist at all is due, not so much to Xinjiang's unique frontier environment, but to two decisive factors: the first involves a certain conceptual understanding; the second involves the problem of vested interests.

The Corps continues to exist as a highly complex and redundant bureaucracy, a society unto itself, an administrative unit possessing provincial-level powers, having every comparable entity except for the Congress of People's Representative and the People's Political Consultative Conference (although all of the Corps' division-level farms and up have their own television stations), and serving as a vast support system for a large number of people. At present, an abrupt dissolution of the Corps seems highly unlikely. This is because the Corps has come to be seen as a tangible affirmation of certain specific historical achievements.

Nonetheless, regarding the continued existence of the Corps, we must consider the following questions:

1. As for the Corps being a deterrent to secession, is it necessary to entrust this task to an armed militia external to the country's formal armed forces? Is the Corps, in its role as a unique social organization, an adequate military deterrent? And is it equipped to carry out this task?

2. If the answers to the above questions are affirmative, how then should we view the ethnic opposition and suspicion that the Corps has, in fact, provoked? How do we weigh the political pros and cons?

3. The Corps clearly has the strong backing of the central government, which trumpets the role of the Corps as a deterrent to secessionism. The implicit assumption is that the central government does not trust non–Han Chinese ethnic minorities. But is this worth the political cost?

4. With problems in Xinjiang attracting increased international attention, it is easy to view the Corps as nothing more than an organized militia of armed migrants. If the Corps is to survive in the long term, how do we address the problem of its identity in modern society?

5. Viewed from any angle, the organizational system of the Corps is grossly incompatible with contemporary Chinese society. Supposing there are no fundamental changes to Xinjiang's internal or external environment, is the continued existence of the Corps really necessary?

Thoughts and Recommendations

1. For both practical and technical reasons, it would be difficult to disband the Corps in the short run, and this would probably breed more problems than it would solve. Nonetheless, it is necessary to begin discussing and making

arrangements for the Corps' gradual withdrawl from the historical stage.

2. While recognizing the Corps' contributions to land reclamation and border security during a unique period in history, it is now appropriate to dial down the propaganda about the role of the Corps in opposing and deterring separatism, because this only serves to undermine national unity—the Corps is distrusted by the Uyghur community, while Uyghurs are distrusted by Han Chinese in the Corps.

3. Assuming that the Corps remains fundamentally intact, move forward with urbanization based on local conditions and considerations. In places where the process of urbanization is complete, pilot programs should be initiated to integrate Corps and local government;

4. Resolving the problem of population drain must begin with land policy. A systematic plan is needed to sort out institutional conflicts about the long-term allocation of land, usage rights, income, and shares between the state, the Corps, its divisions, regimental farms, and individual workers. Only by establishing a clear-cut, permanent relationship between the land and individuals can we resolve the problem of population drain; otherwise, the cost of maintaining the Corps will become exorbitant.

5. The transfer of high-quality local mineral resources to the private sector is not a lasting solution to the Corps' financial predicament. Given the institutional rigidity of the Corps, this seems to run counter to the spirit of reform, and may not be sound economic strategy.

6. The Corps should exercise its political function, as the state propaganda proclaims, of promoting ethnic exchange and ethnic unity. When addressing the issue of population drain, the Corps should remain open to outside perspectives and maximize the benefits of local and regional labor surpluses by encouraging these workers to migrate to underpopulated Corps areas.

7. In comparison to Uyghur rural communities, the Corps has great advantages in agricultural production technology and techniques. The central or local government could appropriate special funds to create and broadcast, on Corps television stations, Uyghur language programs and public service–style broadcasts designed to share this wealth of knowledge. By sharing and spreading its agricultural knowledge and experience with a Uyghur audience, the Corps can help transform traditional, insular production methods and mindsets and make an important contribution to fostering communication and cohesion between different ethnic groups.

VII. Governmental Competence and Credibility

Overview

There is a vast disparity between economic and social development in Xinjiang and in other regions of mainland China. This disparity extends to the official mindset: at all levels of government in Xinjiang, we encounter a mentality that falls far short of what is needed to govern and manage Xinjiang's societal complexities.

The class struggle and dictatorial mindset that died out so long ago in other parts of China (particularly in the economically developed coastal regions) still exists, to varying degrees, in some places in Xinjiang. Compared to other regions of mainland China, Xinjiang retains more aspects of the planned economy: officials at all levels are inclined to be heavy-handed, and local officials have the final say in what crops farmers are allowed to plant. This occurs not only within the Corps: in some areas, it is only within the last year or two that farmers have won the right to manage their own agricultural activities. Uyghur farmers in southern Xinjiang are still in the habit of referring to the township government as "The Commune," because many people don't sense that tremendous changes have transformed China's society.

Xinjiang's cadres and officials have a weak grasp of modern concepts of legality. There is a distinct "generation gap" in the mentality of cadres in Xinjiang's developed cities, such as Urumqi, and their contemporaries in even more developed regions of China. Likewise, there is a "generation gap" in the mindset of cadres in rural southern Xinjiang and cadres in Xinjiang's more developed northern cities. During the July 2009 ethnic unrest, rural cadres from southern Xinjiang were transferred to Urumqi en masse to help maintain order; their behavior was so boorish that even the local cadres in Urumqi were appalled.

The program to transfer laborers from Xinjiang to Shaoguan in Guangdong Province [where the "Shaoguan Incident" of June 25–26, 2009, took place] started out as a positive and worthwhile endeavor.[5] The way in which it was carried out, however, called to mind coercive methods that were more prevalent in the 1980s: home demolitions, forced relocations, land confiscation, and so on. Poor governance at the grassroots level doomed the program from the start and bred a climate of suspicion and resistance.

In southern Xinjiang in particular, Chinese cadres are very nearly regarded as "stand-ins" for all Han Chinese, representatives of an entire race of people. As such, if their methods of governing are unjust or inept, conflicts between citizens and officials can easily escalate into ethnic conflict.

Therefore, we may conclude that the quality of Xinjiang's cadres is a decisive factor in determining how smoothly the government can implement its policies there.

Zhang Chunxian now faces the test of rebuilding the government's image within the community. There are two aspects to this test: the former is restoring government credibility,

---

5   The Shaoguan Incident of June 25–26, 2009, was a violent dispute between Uyghur and Han Chinese migrant workers at a toy factory in Shaoguan, Guangdong Province. The dispute began with allegations of the sexual assault of a Han Chinese woman and escalated into a conflict in which at least two Uyghurs were killed and hundreds injured (witness reports and casualty estimates vary). The Shaoguan incident was likely a contributing factor to the July 2009 ethnic violence in Urumqi.—Editors

while the latter is convincing citizens that they will not be punished for exercising their right to free speech.

Regarding the former: Between the Shaoguan Incident of June 2009 and the syringe attacks later that year, there were all sorts of rumors flying in both the Han Chinese and Uyghur communities. Certainly, this was the result of long-simmering ethnic tensions and mutual distrust, but it also reflected the local government's approach to handling news and information. Over the years, this approach has eroded public trust in the media and made people unwilling to believe anything the government has to say.

Regarding the latter: In Xinjiang's peculiar legal environment, people can be punished just for speaking out—and punished very severely. This pervasive, coercive atmosphere of fear still exists.

Causes

Xinjiang's remoteness, an economy still dominated by centralized planning, social development that lags behind other areas of China, and two decades of political upheaval on its periphery have naturally led to the dictatorial mindset that prevails at all levels of Xinjiang's local government.

In addition, local governments in Xinjiang are tasked with providing jobs to demobilized military officers, which means that a large proportion of Xinjiang's grassroots cadres are former military officers. Long years of indoctrination about being the "first line of defense," combined with military working methods, has given rise to a unique governing style among Xinjiang's lower-level cadres. Particularly in southern Xinjiang, where living and working conditions are difficult, grassroots cadres are selected primarily for their political qualifications and reliability. As for overall mindset and quality of character, these are not even on the list of criteria, and Xinjiang's limited resources make it impossible to provide systematic training for grassroots cadres spread far and wide.

Since 1997, overall society in Xinjiang has been in a state of high alert against "the three forces," thus further strengthening the dictatorial tendencies of Xinjiang's grassroots cadres. When it comes to dealing with societal and ethnic conflicts, they are resolved to do whatever it takes to smother potential conflict as quickly as possible before it can spread.

Thoughts and Recommendations

1. Crackdown on corruption. Official corruption in Xinjiang is far more brazen than in other parts of China, and its methods and nature even more vile. The only way to restore people's confidence in government is to eliminate corruption.

2. Conduct training for all cadres in the areas of legal regulations, effective governance, and civilized law enforcement. Supplement this with various and convenient methods of social supervision and public reporting to enhance and improve awareness among Xinjiang's cadres.

3. Enhance information transparency. Learning from the experiences of more progressive areas of China and allowing local media more latitude to function will create a positive atmosphere that empowers the community and boosts public morale.

4. When transferring or exchanging cadres, focus on sending cadres to (or accepting them from) the southeastern seaboard region, the major metropolises of Beijing, Shanghai, Guangzhou, and similarly developed areas, while reducing the number of cadres from the north. Use the latest ideas and concepts from these developed areas to influence awareness and promote a positive change in local attitudes.

5. When recruiting and promoting cadres or civil servants, focus on quality of character, vision, experience, and other factors, and place less emphasis on political reliability or obedience.

6. At an opportune moment, release a group of intellectuals who have been unfairly detained, unfairly arrested, and

unfairly convicted—for example, Memetjan Abdulla[6] of the China National Radio Uyghur service, or *Xinjiang Economic Daily* reporter Gheyret Niyaz[7] (Niyaz, an intellectual who grew up in a military family, repeatedly tried to warn local authorities of the danger signs before the July 2009 violence in Urumqi). Releasing some of these individuals as a sign of goodwill would send a positive message to the Uyghur community and help to allay some of its pessimism and frustration.

VIII. Han Chinese Chauvinism

Overview

The preamble to the Chinese Constitution once read: "In the struggle to safeguard national unity, we must oppose Han chauvinism, as well as combat ethnic nationalism." In the Mao era, the two phrases "ethnic nationalism" and "Han chauvinism" would often appear together in discussions of ethnic relations, but today the phrase "Han chauvinism" has completely disappeared from everyday conversation.

Our government has always proclaimed its opposition to "Han chauvinism" as well as "ethnic nationalism," yet virtually no one has ever been arrested or removed from office due to "Han chauvinism." Ethnic minorities account for less than 10 percent of China's total population, yet in the seventeen years before the Cultural Revolution, hundreds of thousands were arrested on charges of "ethnic nationalism" in the People's Republic of China.

In reality, Han chauvinism is now more intense and more overt than it has been at any time in the past. Since "opposing

---

6 Arrested in July, 2009, Memetjan Abdulla is serving a life sentence on charges of separatism, disclosing state secrets, and organizing an illegal protest.—Editors

7 Gheyrat Niyaz managed and edited the Uyghur-language news website Uyghurbiz. Arrested in October 2009, he is serving a sentence of fifteen years in prison on charges of endangering state security.—Editors

the three forces" [of terrorism, religious extremism, and separatism] became the main focus of all levels of government in Xinjiang, Han chauvinism has reappeared in the guise of "safeguarding national unity" and "preserving social stability." No one dares to object, of course, or to criticize this emotional outpouring of Han chauvinism, lest they be accused of harboring separatist tendencies. This chauvinism manifests differently among the citizenry and among officials.

In recent years, discrimination against Uyghurs has intensified to such an extent that it has become institutionalized nationwide. Uyghurs routinely face discrimination in employment, passport issuance, rental housing, hotels, travel, and many other areas of life; many domestic airports even have a designated security channel for residents of Xinjiang.

In Xinjiang itself, Uyghurs are frequently the target of derogatory ethnic slurs by Han Chinese, such as "chan-tou"[8] or "wei-zi"[9]. In other areas of mainland China, Uyghurs encounter discriminatory treatment or even outright rejection when trying to register for hotel accommodation; when boarding planes, trains, or other modes of public transport; and even at internet bars and cafes. Often, a service employee will loudly proclaim: "We can't let you register. It's Public Security Bureau policy." Those who have experienced this discrimination range from

---

8 Huang Zhangjin, a Han journalist who grew up in Xinjiang and is a friend of Ilham Tohti, explained the slur in his 2009 essay, "Goodbye, Ilham." "Chan-tou" literally means "wrapped head." It evolved from "chan-hui" to become a slur for the Uyghurs. Uyghur men once wrapped their heads with white cloth. In official documents of the Qing emperors' court, Uyghurs were referred to as "chan-hui" (Muslims with wrapped head), or "sheng hui" (alien Muslims), as opposed to "Han hui" (Han Muslims), or "shu hui" (native Muslims). The term has metamorphosed in contemporary vernacular use, according to Huang, to mean "muddle-headed." Huang Zhangjin, "Goodbye, Ilham," English translation published February 16, 2021, chinadigitaltimes. net.—Editors

9 "Wei" literally means "Uyghur"; "zi" is a common Chinese suffix without lexical meaning. But "wei-zi" has a condescending, dismissive tone to it.—Editors

students and manual laborers to high-ranking provincial officials and eminent scholars. As for online discussion, it is even more extreme: self-proclaimed "imperial Han" lobbing insults at Xinjiang's "barbarian" ethnic minorities are ubiquitous online.

Han chauvinism in official circles, on the other hand, tends to manifest itself in certain turns of phrase, stock expressions that the speaker uses unquestioningly. Phrases such as "*Yan-Huang zisun*" ("descendants of Yan Di and Huang Di"), "*long de chuanren*" ("descendants of the dragon"), "*Huaxia er-nu*" ("sons and daughters of Cathay") are commonly used to invoke the Han Chinese people in their totality, but if a Uyghur refers to their forebear Oghuz Khan or a "wolf totem," it is thought to be fraught with secessionist implications. Moreover, after the July 2009 ethnic unrest in Urumqi, every branch of every governmental organization in Xinjiang organized study sessions designed to refute the "parochial" view that "Xinjiang belongs to the Uyghurs of Xinjiang." The speakers and scholars at these meetings often claimed that, in fact, it was the Han Chinese forbearers who arrived in Xinjiang before the Uyghur forbearers did, thus employing logic identical to the logic of the claim they were attempting to refute. Appearing as they did in an official capacity, these speakers and scholars were utterly counterproductive.

Incidents such as the aforementioned make Uyghurs feel that society is becoming increasingly unjust and disrespectful of their culture and their feelings.

These slights pale in comparison to the pain and inconvenience ordinary Uyghurs suffer when using public services. To register for an identity card, for example, one is required to fill in a form with one's personal information. With no consideration for the majority of Uyghurs who do not understand Chinese, the form only provides one column heading for "Chinese name." Even if one were to write in Pinyin the Chinese transliteration of one's Uyghur name, the form is nearly impossible to fill out because it does not take into account differences in Uyghur naming conventions. Since census registration was digitized, some local governments have introduced policies that force Uyghurs to choose from a list of commonly used names; if their names are not on the list, they are not allowed to register.

A more serious problem is the Uyghur community's growing fear of the government's increasingly chauvinistic ethnic policies. The government's sharp curtailing of bilingual education and Uyghur cultural enterprises has led many in the Uyghur community to feel that official ethnic policy is beginning to look like forced assimilation. In many public forums, particularly on the internet, it is not difficult to find people openly discussing a point of view common among Han Chinese: that the only way to solve Xinjiang's ethnic problems is to accelerate Uyghur assimilation.

The recent surge in theoretical inquiries that masquerade as critiques of national ethnic policy while negating the principle of regional ethnic autonomy and opposing updated concepts of ethnicity give the impression that virulent Han chauvinism has entered mainstream public discourse. Within the Uyghur community, this has provoked intense fear and a sense of impending crisis, and has severely shaken the Uyghur sense of national identity.

The natural merging of ethnicities and the creation of societies in which diverse ethnic cultures can coexist and learn from one another is an unstoppable historical trend that no one will really oppose, but a fear of forced assimilationist policies rooted in Han chauvinism has prompted more and more Uyghurs to become suspicious of Chinese language education and *Nei-Gao-Ban* [the Chinese acronym for "Inland Xinjiang Senior High School Classes," which are elite courses designed to prepare minority students for entry into prestigious Chinese universities]. These doubts and fears have led many Uyghurs to adopt a form of silent resistance by privately turning back to traditional culture, religious worship, and a strengthened sense of ethnic identity.

Thoughts and Recommendations

1. Enact policies that implement and respect regional ethnic autonomy; respect and protect the existing ethnic and cultural diversity and peaceful co-existence.

2. To combat openly discriminatory speech and behavior, we should take our cues from internationally accepted methods and standards: draft detailed prohibitions; gradually establish a legal and regulatory framework that protects the legitimate rights of minorities and forbids all forms of status discrimination (including ethnic discrimination); use legal means to safeguard the legitimate rights and interests of minorities in employment, public services, and the cultural sphere; and eliminate forms of casual ethnic discrimination. On this basis, we can transform the culture and habits of an entire society, creating a more "politically correct" value system against discrimination.

3. The government should organize systematic research and discussion among experts and scholars to determine which commonly used official phrases are most likely to be misconstrued or wound the feelings of ethnic minorities. Such discussion could be a form of social critique, a way of combatting unconscious racial bias in our speech. For example, describing the Han Chinese people as being uniformly "black haired," "black eyed," and "yellow skinned" would, in the West, be considered a form of overt racial propagandizing inappropriate to public discourse.

4. The government should re-examine and reflect on the role of Han Chinese chauvinism and ethnic nationalism in Chinese society. When dealing with ethnic issues, it is not fair to stress only minority chauvinism and ethnic separatism, while completely ignoring the issue of Han chauvinism. At the very least, the government should allow citizens to freely discuss and criticize both Han chauvinism and ethnic extremism. For China's future as a multiethnic and multicultural nation, and as a rising international

power, the strong strains of Han chauvinism and ethnic nationalism in today's mainstream Chinese society are not a sign of healthy attitudes.

5. In theory, the People's Republic of China is supposed to be comprised of fifty-six different ethnicities. Thus, the terms "overseas Chinese" or "Chinese diaspora" should refer not only to people of Han Chinese lineage, but also to people of other lineages as well. In fact, if the government treated all overseas people with ancestral ties to China even-handedly, the results might well amaze. For example, more than a year ago, the Chinese Embassy in Pakistan began to reach out to the local Uyghur diaspora community: as a result, Pakistani exchange students of Uyghur lineage could soon be heard on Beijing university campuses proclaiming themselves as "overseas Chinese" and taking great pride in their contributions to their ancestral land— whereas in the past, the term "overseas Chinese" was never used to describe diaspora Uyghurs, because it seemed to refer specifically to people of Han Chinese descent.

IX. Ethnic Regional Autonomy and Anti-separatism

Overview

Upon the founding of the People's Republic of China, China created a set of clear-cut national policies based on the principles of regional ethnic autonomy and ethnic equality, backed by the Chinese Constitution, the Regional Ethnic Autonomy Law, and a variety of other legal mechanisms. Not only was this a fundamental leap forward for China, a vast improvement over the old system, it was also well ahead of many Western countries at the time. China's system of regional ethnic autonomy was based on a fair distribution of dignity and power; it was meant to be an integrated institutional mechanism capable of balancing the needs of the state with the needs of ethnic peoples, but it has never been carried out and implemented properly.

Although the Regional Ethnic Autonomy Law was promulgated as a basic law nearly thirty years ago, there still are no regional-level regulations governing its implementation. The system of regional ethnic autonomy is a story of years of accumulated promises—promises that have, noticeably, not yet been honored.

There are a variety of reasons why regional ethnic autonomy has never been truly implemented: cultural and economic factors, the unique political climate of the times, and other factors. The Uyghur community was never particularly vocal about this nonimplementation, partly because of a lack of awareness or knowledge about their basic rights, and partly because they never felt that their legitimate rights and interests had been seriously undermined.

But over the last decade or two, at least in Xinjiang, the purely nominal nature of regional ethnic autonomy has become an increasingly serious problem. Legislative attempts to implement true regional ethnic autonomy have stalled or made no headway, which means that provisions contained in the Chinese Constitution and the Regional Ethnic Autonomy Law—both of which include clear stipulations regarding minority employment, cultural protection, cadre functions, religious belief, and other issues—are impossible to enforce. Ignoring the stipulations of China's Regional Ethnic Autonomy Law has led to the ethnic problems we discussed earlier; it is also the reason that Uyghur rights and interests have not received due legal protection.

Implementing and enforcing rules and regulations related to regional ethnic autonomy has been a difficult task from the beginning, but now there is a new problem that makes the future of ethnic autonomy even more complicated and uncertain.

Today, the discussion is not about how to implement regional ethnic autonomy, but about whether or not to abolish it. This is particularly true since the occurrence of ethnic strife in Lhasa in 2008 and in Urumqi in 2009. A group of scholars led by Ma Rong and Yang Shengming, in re-examining ethnic policies and the dissolution of the former Soviet Union, have begun to argue openly against the concept of regional ethnic autonomy. Furthermore, in the name of eradicating ethnic separatist ideology, they have put forward a viewpoint that seems akin to "abolishing the idea of ethnicity altogether."

At a time when even ethnologists are publicly questioning the regional autonomy provisions of the Chinese Constitution, rare are those who dare to publicly stand up for the principle of regional ethnic autonomy, much less demand the full implementation of the Regional Ethnic Autonomy Law. This will lead to the following effect: the public will come to believe that it is the intent of the government to abolish regional ethnic autonomy, and they will take it as a public expression of support for forced assimilation. And in today's climate, anyone who dares to openly discuss implementing ethnic autonomy is automatically perceived as advocating ethnic separatism.

When academia speaks with a single voice, that voice does not necessarily reflect social reality. For example, before the 2009 ethnic unrest in Urumqi, Yang Shengming's published survey on ethnic problems in Xinjiang claimed that Uyghurs had a stronger sense of national identity than even Han Chinese, and that Uyghurs and Han Chinese showed similarly high levels of support for inter-ethnic marriage. The report concluded that the idea that Xinjiang had serious ethnic problems was "an alarmist viewpoint." But our survey showed the exact opposite: the outlook for national identity in the Uyghur community was not optimistic, and every ethnic group, in fact, seemed to oppose and resist inter-ethnic marriage.

The lack of public voices supporting the protection and implementation of regional ethnic autonomy is actually quite frightening, because China's ethnic minorities are crying out for genuine ethnic autonomy. If regional ethnic autonomy is not an option, only two possible scenarios remain: abolishing ethnic autonomy and enforcing assimilation, or ethnic independence movements.

Doing away with regional ethnic autonomy under the mantle of opposing separatism is an extremely dangerous idea because it will nudge more and more ethnic minorities from hopelessness into irrational support for independence movements. The true threat to China's national unity and integrity is not ethnic autonomy: it is the prospect of abolishing ethnic autonomy.

To some extent, countering secessionism in Xinjiang is a race between the full implementation of regional ethnic autonomy and the forces of ethnic separatism.

Thoughts

Thus far, the path to addressing and resolving ethnic relations in multiethnic nations has involved some form of regional autonomy. Almost without exception, this has been the case in multiethnic nations formed by historical circumstance (typified by Switzerland, Spain, Belgium, Britain, and France, as well as other European countries), and in multiethnic and multicultural nations formed through immigration (such as the French-speaking areas of Canada).

Among the rare exceptions are the United States, Malaysia (with its Chinese immigrants), and a few other nations. In these nations, because multiple ethnicities and cultures later began to merge, they never formed into ethnic enclaves or regions.

The prescription that Ma Rong and other scholars are recommending for China today is patently mistaken and dangerous when they repeatedly emphasize the American experiences as a model without respecting the fact that China's experiences and national conditions are vastly different from those of the United States.

Separatism exists in most every corner of the globe. Among advanced Western nations, France has the Corsican problem, the British have the dispute over Northern Ireland, Spain has the Basque and Catalan problems, Canada has the Quebec separatist movement, Japan has the Ryukyu Islands independence movement . . . even the United States has a few dozen separatist organizations.

No country has found a way to completely eliminate separatism. But through economic development, the implementation of civil rights, systemic design and the use of legal means, some have consistently managed to marginalize and neutralize separatist movements, while at the same time enhancing solidarity, safeguarding national unity, and mitigating the pressures of globalization. There are many successful examples to choose from.

Perhaps the most worthwhile example is Spain. In the late 1970s, after Spain bid farewell to authoritarianism, the Basque and Catalan separatist movements broke out. Fueled by stark ethnic and linguistic differences, the Basque separatist movement enjoyed nearly unanimous support among the Basque people, and extremist separatist groups carried out constant attacks. In October 1979, referenda on the Statute of Autonomy that balanced the interests of the various parties were held in the two restive regions (Catalan and Basque) and each gained over 90 percent approval. Among today's Basques (the group with the most serious separatist tendencies) 64 percent oppose independence; in Catalonia, the figure is as high as 80 percent.

Chinese scholars frequently regard Yugoslavia as a case study in secessionism, but few people draw the correct lesson: although the separatist tendencies of ethnic peoples in Yugoslavia were far less serious than in Spain, the dominant ethnic group, the Serbs, cared less about the nation's territorial integrity than they did about competing with other ethnic groups for a bigger slice of the national pie. Fanatical Serbian nationalism played a destructive role in Yugoslavia's dissolution.

The most fundamental solution to Xinjiang's ethnic problem is to enforce Chinese constitutional provisions regarding regional ethnic autonomy and to try to strike a balance between ethnic autonomy and national unity.

Recommendations

1. As soon as possible, promulgate and implement the statute of autonomy in the Xinjiang Uyghur Autonomous Region and the detailed rules for the implementation of the existing Law of the People's Republic of China on Regional Ethnic Autonomy in order to implement the law by establishing an institutional framework that provides sound legal foundations for regional ethnic autonomy in China.

   The statute of autonomy would be the most fundamental embodiment of the right of self-determination in China's ethnic autonomous regions. Yet as of now, not a single statute of autonomy has been put forward to protect autonomous government in the Xinjiang Uyghur Autonomous Region or the five autonomous prefectures and six autonomous counties under its jurisdiction. In contrast, in the Yanbian Korean Autonomous Prefecture, legislative work on provisions for ethnic autonomy was complete by the mid 1980s. Yanbian can be regarded as China's most successful example of implementing regional ethnic autonomy.

2. Allow discussion and public dialogue on the subject of implementing regional ethnic autonomy while also safeguarding national unity. In practical terms, this is a necessary precondition to seeking equilibrium between national unity and regional ethnic autonomy in Xinjiang.

3. The current system of government should establish at least one benchmark for the progressive implementation of regional ethnic autonomy in Xinjiang. Such a benchmark would help to improve on the status quo on such issues as Uyghur employment, cultural protection, appointment of cadres, and religious practice, and would help to greatly reduce current levels of ethnic resentment and strife.

   Finally, when crafting policies designed to aid Xinjiang, the central government should cease favoring the economic sphere at the expense of the political and cultural spheres.

It should also avoid unilateral "financial infusions" that ignore the local economy, particularly those that overlook the local Uyghur socio-economic support system. Currently, government aid to Xinjiang revolves around bringing in big business and big capital from other parts of mainland China, but offers few opportunities for local capital or minority-owned capital. Some places in Xinjiang have already experienced a crowding-out effect, with outside capital pushing out local capital; we should remain vigilant to such signals. Because they have no positive effect on local employment, and can even directly harm the interests of local industry and commerce, today's government aid policies in Xinjiang will have even more negative consequences than similar wasteful and ineffective policies in Tibet (see Jin Wei's *Aid Policies and Tibetan Economic Development*).

Statements

"I Don't Have Too Many Good Days Ahead of Me"

A Statement to the Radio Free Asia Uyghur Service, July 24, 2013

There is a lot of tension around here. In the past few days, I have been under constant surveillance by police vehicles and national security police officers. I have been under heavy supervision.

Furthermore, anyone I have interacted with recently, regardless of ethnicity, Uyghur or Han Chinese, has had to suffer through interrogations by the government. I have realized that I don't have too many good days ahead of me, and I have a feeling that they [the Chinese government] may not have the best intentions in dealing with my situation. Therefore, I feel that it is necessary for me to leave a few words behind before I no longer have the ability to do so.

Medical Examination

First, I would like to emphasize that currently, there are no physical marks or bruises on my body. About two months ago, the school [Central University for Nationalities] performed physical examinations on all the teachers, including myself. The results of my physical examinations have been recorded on their computers and were sent to all major hospitals in Beijing. They should be available in their archives. I am currently very healthy and do not have any illnesses.

The last time I fell ill was after I was beaten by a few national security officers at the airport on February 2, 2013.

The police officers punched my heart at the time, and after the incident I had chest pains whenever I felt tired. However, I no longer feel the chest pains and I am in perfectly healthy condition.

If I do pass away in the near future, know that it is not because of natural illness and it certainly will not be suicide. I am a Uyghur, a father, and a righteous man. I do not commend suicide and neither does the Uyghur culture. Therefore it is impossible that I will ever commit suicide. This is my first point.

Lawyer

Second, I do not want an appointed lawyer and I will never accept an appointed lawyer under any circumstances. I have my own lawyer whom [the Tibetan writer Tsering] Woeser knows. Other people are aware of this as well.

False Confession

Third, I will never say anything that is against my morals and principles, nor will I ever say anything that may harm my people [the Uyghurs]. If I say anything that deviates from my morals after my arrest, know that those are not my words. Any word that is at conflict with my morals or brings harm to the Uyghur people would most likely have been fabricated by the Chinese government.

The only possibility of my uttering such words would be due to drugs or other substances intended to coerce a false confession. Regardless of the interrogation strategy or the torture method, regardless of what body parts I am about to lose, know that I will never speak words that will work against the interest of the Uyghurs, nor will I ever betray the Uyghurs. The only way I may utter such words is under abnormal circumstances. When I say "abnormal," I am referring to an abnormal state of mind, perhaps influenced by drugs.

Peaceful Path

My fourth point is that I have never associated myself with a terrorist organization or a foreign-based group. The path I have pursued all along is an honorable and a peaceful path. I have relied only on pen and paper to diplomatically request human rights, legal rights, and autonomous regional rights for the Uyghurs.

I have relentlessly appealed for equality for Uyghurs in regards to their individuality, religion, and culture. I have persistently demanded justice from the Chinese government. However, I have never pursued a violent route and I have never joined a group that utilized violence.

I have never started an organization, but I have attracted a number of friends and supporters, both Uyghur and Han Chinese, who share my vision. It would be absolutely unreasonable of the PRC government to use this fact against me. The only things I have ever wanted and requested are human rights, legal rights, autonomous regional rights, and equality. Uyghurs should be able to receive the same respect given to the Chinese, and they should also have the ability to preserve their dignity. This is my fourth point.

I will never view myself as a criminal, and I feel that it is necessary for me to make these points.

Security

Many of my friends have been arrested lately. The number of police officers around me has been gradually increased. They have been watching me even on school campus. I have never been surrounded by this many police officers, even around the July 5th Incident in 2009.

Since July of this year [2013], I have not been able to communicate as much with journalists and reporters abroad. Since the website (Uyghurbiz.net) attracts a lot of visitors and activities, the Chinese government is not pleased with it either. I am almost certain that their intentions are corrupt this time, but I would like to say that mine are not. I have always led by example through advocating for diplomatic and peaceful ways to request justice and equality. I believe that Beijing is the ideal place for education, and I believe that this city is a key to achieving equality and justice.

Without the understanding and support of all of the 1.3 billion people in China, it would be extremely difficult for us to achieve our human rights goals. One of my foremost objectives so far has been to introduce and explain who we really are to the Han Chinese population, and this is how I have gained so many friends and supporters who are Han Chinese.

I have never spoken like this before, but I am almost certain that the Chinese government is trying to get rid of me this time.

Xinjiang Government

I remember that three years ago I had refused to comment about my opinions of Zhang Chunxian [the ruling Chinese Communist Party secretary of the Xinjiang Uyghur Autonomous Region]. However, I have expressed my thoughts and opinions about him recently through my writings and lectures and through letters I have written. I am certain that Zhang Chunxian wasn't very happy about what I had to say. I have recently received "communications," and I must say that I don't feel very safe at the moment. Please save this conversation from today and be sure to keep it until you need to release it, when it is necessary.

"My Outcries Are for My People and, Even More, for the Future of China"

Statement on September 24, 2014, after receiving a life sentence for "separatist" crimes

My outcries are for my people and, even more, for the future of China.

Before entering prison, I kept worrying I wouldn't be able to deal with the harshness inside. I worried I would betray my conscience, career, friends, and family. I made it!

The upcoming life in prison is not something I've experienced, but it will nonetheless become our life and my own experience. I don't know how long my life can go on. I have courage; I will not be fragile. If you hear news that I mutilated or killed myself, you can be certain it is made up.

After seeing the judgment against me, contrary to what people may think, I now think I have a more important duty to bear.

Even though I have departed, I still live in anticipation of the sun and the future. I am convinced that China will become better and that the constitutional rights of the Uyghur people will, one day, be honored.

Peace is a heavenly gift to the Uyghur and Han people. Only peace and good will can create a common interest.

I wear my shackles twenty-four hours a day, and was only allowed physical exercise for three hours out of the last eight months. My cell mates are eight sentenced Han prisoners. These are fairly harsh conditions. However, I count myself fortunate when I look at what has happened to my students and other Uyghurs accused of separatist crimes. I had my own Han lawyer whom I appointed to defend me, and my family was allowed to attend my trial. I was able to say what I wanted to say. I hope that, through my case, rule of law in Xinjiang can improve, even if it is only a baby step.

After yesterday's sentencing, I slept better than I ever did in the eight months [of my detention]. I never realized I had this in me. The only thing is, don't tell my old mother what has happened. Tell my family to tell her that it's only a five-year sentence. Last night, in the cell next door, Parhat Halmurat [a student of Ilham's and an editor of the Uyghurbiz website] slammed himself against the door and cried out loud. I heard the sound of shackles, nonstop, as they were taken to interrogations. Maybe my students have been sentenced too.

[To his wife]: My love, for the sake of our children, please be strong and don't cry! In a future not too far away, we will be in each other's arms once more. Take care of yourself! Love, Ilham.

Interviews

The Watchman of the Uyghur People

An interview conducted by Shohret Nijat[1] on November 29, 2008, at Ilham Tohti's home in Beijing.

Shohret Nijat (SN): A few friends of yours from Xinjiang came to Beijing last week—were you happy to see them?

Ilham: Yes, we had a gathering!

SN: Even though everyone hadn't met for so long, all the feelings were there.

Ilham: Of course—most of them were my friends from school and university. Whenever we're together we never run out of things to talk about.

SN: What did you talk about?

Ilham: Everything. We told stories from our youth—whenever we recall those days, the blood really starts pumping. I feel that the kids of that generation have a strong sense of responsibility. We dare to be at the forefront and have a certain verve. The generation of Uyghur kids today, on the other hand, is not the same.

SN: Are you saying that the current generation of Uyghur young people doesn't have a sense of responsibility? That they lack the verve and vigor you speak of?

Ilham: Yes. The kids today are a bit selfish, and they don't have much self-confidence.

---

1   Shohret Nijat is one of the seven students charged with involvement in the Uyghurbiz.net website; he was tried and sentenced during a secret trial held in November 2014. The seven students received sentences of between three to eight years in prison. It's unclear where they are now held.—Editors

SN: Why do you think that is?

Ilham: What you lack today is the ability to think about things philosophically. It's a crucial ability. You've gradually become estranged from the culture and history of your own people. What parents teach their children at home is also a huge issue. These days parents are likely to tell their kids to "look after yourself and mind your own business." Our ancestors didn't think like that. A portion of farming households in southern Xinjiang have preserved good traditions. For example, they'll go out themselves and sweep the sidewalk. The kids don't litter, even when there are no garbage bins around. We never used to be a selfish people. What we lack is a transition to modernity.

The issues we now face need to be borne, to a degree, by the current generation of young people: we don't look after ourselves as a people, and as a people we are having a crisis. Maybe it's because I'm a teacher, but when I see the young Uyghur students today, I really become anxious. It's as though you've lost the sense of responsibility for suffering and thinking about our people. Most of your time is wasted in online games and chat rooms.

SN: Isn't this a whole social malady? Children from the majority ethnicity, the Han people, are the same, aren't they?

Ilham: Even though there are all sorts of comments in society about the millennial generation of the Han, I actually think their millennials are quite exceptional. They're more capable than the generation before. On the other hand, our young people are failing to carry on our culture, and we're losing the better parts of our own traditions. We seem lost as a people. Uyghurs are facing a "cultural crisis." Even though Han people are also facing their own cultural crisis, they're still doing better than us—at the very least, their intellectual class is quite outstanding compared to ours.

SN: Maybe, as in your generation, there aren't many in our cohort who dare to speak out.

Ilham: Indeed. Now it's not merely a question of whether we dare or want to speak up—the entire social and political environment in Xinjiang is completely different to how it was back then. At the very least, when we were growing up, teachers could speak about the history and culture of our people in class. Now, that happens very little. There's no room for expression or research either. The environment for Uyghurs to survive and develop socially is extremely dire.

At University, I Got the Nickname "News for Reference"[2]

SN: When you left Xinjiang and moved to the interior for university, was it difficult for you academically?

Ilham: Back then I matriculated because I had exceptionally high grades. I scored 68 in mathematics on the national college entrance test. It was pretty decent where I came from, but when I got to university [in Changchun, Jilin province], I discovered that among Han students, the lowest score was 99. During middle school I was a "three good" student [as evaluated ideologically, educationally, and physically], and I was always ranked among the best. But in university I was surrounded by better students, and I felt the gulf. Also, in my first year, first semester, I failed a course.

SN: Presumably this had a big impact on you at the time?

Ilham: That's for sure. I always worked hard in my studies. After I flunked the class, I didn't lose heart. I reflected, and I even pinned up a poem above my bed. I forget the exact lines, but it was basically encouraging me to study in earnest, and that I'd come to study in order to represent my people, so I just couldn't fall behind. I never slacked off. I'd be at the library

---

2 *Cankao Xiaoxi*, or *News for Reference*, is a daily published by China's state news agency, Xinhua. It carefully selects articles from world media and translates them into Chinese. Before the 1980s, it was the only channel enabling the Chinese public to get a glimpse of the outside world.—Editors

all the time, and worked so hard that at one point I only weighed 50 kilograms.

At university I got the nickname "Reference News." I sought knowledge like I was quenching a thirst. I went to the library and read all the newspapers of the day, and then the magazines, and then the books in my area of specialty. I knew where they were, and librarians would let me into restricted areas to read. The library closed at 9:00 p.m., but then I'd head to the self-study room to keep reading. I remember an essay I wrote in university which I sent, as a kind of experiment, to *Guangming Daily*'s theoretical page—amazingly, they published it. Even my teachers began to look at me differently.

SN: In those four years, how many times did you go back home?

Ilham: Not once. I wanted to stay at school, read more books, and improve my language.

SN: What would you do on summer and during winter breaks?

Ilham: I studied English, among other things. At that point my English wasn't bad. I carried a little radio around with me all the time to improve my Mandarin as well.

SN: Why didn't you choose to go straight home after graduation?

Ilham: I was afraid that if I went home there would be nothing to do. I was afraid that there was no use for me in Xinjiang. I also had misgivings, because I took part in pro-democracy demonstrations in 1985 and 1989.

SN: So you chose to study further?

Ilham: That's right. For my graduate studies, I was accepted into Minzu University of China in Beijing, studying economics. Then in South Korea I studied economic policy, but I didn't finish the degree.

SN: Why is that?

Ilham: The Ghulja Incident[3] happened around then. But I didn't

---

3 Also known as the Ghulja Massacre, in early February 1997; an estimated 100 or more peaceful Uyghur protesters were killed by gunfire in the city of Ghulja, as the authorities put down a protest against the mass execution of Uyghur activists and restrictions on Uyghur culture.—Editors

know about it in South Korea. I was the first Uyghur student in South Korea. A reporter from SBS interviewed me, asking me for my thoughts. After that, a Korean newspaper frequently solicited op-ed articles. I wrote about Uyghur culture, customs, the Three Districts Revolution (三区革命),[4] ethnic regional autonomy, and so on. But because of a range of political, financial, and personal reasons, I didn't get the PhD degree.

SN: Most of your school friends went on to exchange programs overseas, obtaining doctoral degrees, and some staying there—but for a variety of reasons, you didn't realize this wish.

Ilham: Not quite. But when we get together, they all understand my choices. All in my generation think of ourselves as warriors.

The Plight of Uyghur Education in Xinjiang

SN: For a long time there has been a two-faction split among the educated class of Uyghurs: those who take national college entrance exams in Mandarin (*min-kao-han*) and those in Uyghur (*min-kao-min*). Each group rejects the other.

Ilham: First, I took the exams in the Uyghur language. Now, through study, I can communicate and write articles fluently in Chinese. In the "*min-kao-min*" system, ethnic students are able to learn about their own language, history, and culture. They are educated this way from a young age, and for kids this is key to developing self-awareness and character at a young age. The "*min-kao-han*" system leads to serious alienation from the native culture. Those who took the "*min-kao-han*" track should much more take on the task of explaining their native culture to the Han, but they haven't

---

4   An independence movement led by Uyghur rebels in northern Xinjiang, supported by the Soviet Union, in the regions of Ili, Tarbaghatai, and Altai in the mid-1940s.—Editors

done that. The young generation, who are mostly *min-kao-han*, thinks that its horizons have been broadened, and that you have a more integrated quality than *min-kao-min*, but you haven't done what you should have.

SN: Furthermore, now the "bilingual" education implemented in Xinjiang has pushed the *min-kao-min* system into a crisis.

Ilham: This is indeed a problem. Admittedly, bilingual education is a good thing—but the form of it being practiced now in Xinjiang is not the same thing the government has been advocating. I once did an investigation of this, and the leaders I know, whether Han or Uyghur, in the local education department are also very concerned—they're quite aware that there are problems. For example, in a certain place in southern Xinjiang, they were unable to find a Mandarin teacher, so they went to a brick factory and grabbed a migrant worker. The education bureau chief, who was Han, was furious at this. From a certain perspective, what's happening now in Xinjiang is a Great Cultural Revolution that is destroying the indigenous culture. Even though the propaganda about bilingual education is that it's great for minority students, in the future a great number of problems are going to surface.

SN: Though bilingual education and encouraging minority students to study Mandarin is a good thing, why has the effect been opposite to that portrayed by the government?

Ilham: Bilingual education around the world is a mature field with a wealth of experience in both success and failure. What's being practiced now in Xinjiang is not entirely bilingual education. For instance, in ethnic-language elementary schools nowadays they don't teach the alphabet of the mother tongue until the fourth grade; there are schools in which the kids aren't allowed to communicate in their own ethnic language. Teachers call out and criticize students who don't speak Mandarin. The result of this is that many students go home and speak to their parents in Mandarin. Bilingual education shouldn't be built on a foundation of harming native languages and cultures, under the slogan of "mother-tongue education is the foundation; foreign-language education is the pillar; bilingual education is the path." For the bilingual education to be actually welcomed by the public, the mother tongue can't be marginalized and neglected.

SN: It's not merely bilingual education that is a sham; in Xinjiang, the entire education system for peoples other than Han has seen a decline from earlier eras.

Ilham: Our modern education used to be just as good as that in the rest of China. If you examine Uyghur education history, you'll see. Uyghur modernizing educators used to invite teachers from Turkey, Tajikistan, and Tashkent [the capital of Uzbekistan]. Before China's interior was teaching geography, we had this curriculum established. We also taught several branches of mathematics, including geometry and algebra. In the 1930s and 1940s we established the first accounting school in China at Ili; the first school for animal husbandry was also founded in Xinjiang by Uyghurs. There were also the old leaders; Burhan Shahidi[5] graduated from Berlin University, while Saifuddin Azizi[6] and others were graduates of well-known

---

5 Burhan Shahidi (1894–1989) was a prominent Uyghur leader who studied in Germany and, during the era of the Republic of China, assumed various government positions, including chairman of Xinjiang Provincial Government, beginning in January 1949. In December 1949, he became Chairman of the Xinjiang Provincial People's Government under the new regime led by the Chinese Communist Party. During the Cultural Revolution from the 1960s to 1970s, he was accused of being a collaborator and imprisoned for eight years. He was later described as an "outstanding representative of the Uyghur people" by the CCP's official biography of him. "The life of Comrade Burhan," cpc.people.com.cn.

6 Saifuddin Azizi (1915–2003), also known as Seypidin Azizi, was a prominent Uyghur leader. He grew up in Xinjiang and was educated in the Soviet Union. In 1949 he become a Communist Party member, and from 1955 to 1967, succeeding Burhan Shahidi, and again from 1972 to 1978, he was the Chairman of the Xinjiang Uyghur Autonomous Region. He held the position of Vice Chairman of the National People's Congress in Beijing for nearly four decades, from the 1950s to the 1990s, and he was a Vice Chairman of the Chinese People's Political Consultative Conference from 1993 to 1998.

Soviet universities and colleges. They were highly educated and knowledgeable. Nowadays, you can count the number of these types of leaders on your fingers. A solid education in the humanities is crucial for any people. But now, the transmission of culture and education among our people has been severely damaged. Ethnic pedagogy in Xinjiang is in a terrible state.

SN: Should the intellectuals of our people bear some responsibility for this?

Ilham: Intellectuals are indeed a backbone of a people. But as a people we've suffered so much control and restriction. After the collapse of the Soviet Union in 1991, China grew vigilant about the Central Asian region. A consequence of this was that its policies toward Uyghurs in Xinjiang, especially toward the Uyghur educated class, became stricter and stricter.

SN: The difficulties in ethnic education have also led to a range of social problems.

Ilham: In the society we had before, there was no such thing as AIDS, street urchins, theft, and other such social problems. A great part of the old Silk Road stretched through Xinjiang, and these paths were unobstructed and clear. Uyghurs were never bandits. Also, for instance, the drug problem. When the entire society was enveloped in opium smoke, Uyghurs never suffered this problem. In fact, the watershed year for drugs as a serious social problem in Xinjiang was 1991. Prior to 1991, there were very few people who smoked and drank. After that, living conditions for Uyghurs began to get worse and worse, and drug problems got out of control. Especially after 1997, I found that a lot of young people from Ili came to the Weigong Cun and Ganjia Kou areas in Beijing and they stole from people and also traded drugs.

RFA reported in 2017 that Saifuddin's books were removed from bookstores in Xinjiang per an internal Party directive: "Xinjiang Authorities Ban Books by Uyghur Former Chairman of Region," August 14, 2017, Radio Free Asia, rfa.org.

The Importance of "Uyghurbiz" as a Platform

SN: I heard about you through an article that appeared in *Phoenix Weekly*, vol. 17, 2007, about street urchins from Xinjiang. The article cited some of the research you'd done.

Ilham: Actually, the *Phoenix Weekly* reporter worked with Uyghurbiz staff to put that piece together.

SN: It's very rare to see articles like that, even among Uyghurs, reporting on social problems in Xinjiang.

Ilham: I think it's because Uyghur society finds it hard to accept. If we as a people expose ourselves like that, some will be angry, saying, "Why are you saying all these bad things about us?"

SN: Are there people among our group who don't want to forthrightly face our failings?

Ilham: I've seen some nativist Uyghur websites where Uyghurs themselves are avoiding these issues. But we're influencing them. The most important thing Uyghurbiz is doing is working hard to teach young Uyghur people that they should dare to speak the truth.

SN: Is daring to speak the truth the same as simply complaining?

Ilham: In Uyghur society, resigning oneself to adversity and not caring about other people has already become an entrenched social phenomenon. The "speaking" I'm referring to is about telling others about our own history, culture, who we are, the conditions of our ethnic regions, the employment situation of young people, and so on. Some people think that Uyghurbiz is just about giving people with ethnic sentiments a space online to sound off. But that's not what it's about. There needs to be a platform for people to make their feelings known, and every people has the right to express their own ideas and rights.

SN: Is that your goal in setting up Uyghurbiz?

Ilham: That's right. I really think Uyghurbiz is an important platform. We're doing our best right now to let every corner of the world understand the Xinjiang and Uyghur issue. We're trying to change the prejudicial views that people have toward

Uyghurs. Our efforts have seen some preliminary results. A number of well-known publications inside and outside China have republished some of the high-quality articles we posted to the website.

SN: Did you encounter any interference when first setting up the website?

Ilham: There were obstacles. Whether we could even use the word "Uyghur" was a point of contention. I was frequently summoned and questioned by police. But despite the obstacles, we've been moving forward.

SN: Are you not afraid?

Ilham: I once told the relevant organs that even if they lock me up for twenty years, it'll be the same whether I'm in jail or not. On the outside, I'm very pained; inside jail, maybe it'll actually be easier. I acknowledge the fact that I'm a supporter of ethnic self-determination. But even more than that, I'm a Chinese patriot. What we want to do is open channels of communication, to have society progress peacefully.

SN: Uyghurbiz has been running for nearly three years. What has its impact been?

Ilham: There's been impact, and the name recognition of the website itself has slowly been on the rise. Our click-throughs have been growing steadily year by year, which is quite rare in China when it comes to websites that introduce and discuss minority ethnicity issues. Even though Uyghurbiz is a tiny platform, it has in fact led to some changes. For instance, if you search "Uyghur" online now, our website is among the first three results. Our website is also used as study material for students in universities outside China.

SN: How about among Uyghurs?

Ilham: I'm not sure about working-class folks, but the influence among intellectuals has been quite significant. Most of our registered users at the moment are Uyghur intellectuals, students, and those of other minority ethnicities who are interested in Uyghur issues. Our collective efforts have also led

to the government paying attention to some of the social problems we've pointed out—for instance, the problem of street
kids. This word hadn't even appeared on the Chinese internet
until we began using it; you could say that we're the first ones
to introduce this concept.

SN: Was the street kid issue something that Uyghurbiz began to
focus on as soon as it was established?

Ilham: It was one or two months after the website went live. At
the time you'd go online and all the news about Xinjiang street
kids was entirely negative—that they're thieves and so on. We
thought that this was just unacceptable, so we began gathering materials and really investigating the matter on the ground.
As a result we set up a page specifically focused on this issue.

SN: Street kids are very common in southern Xinjiang. Why is that?

Ilham: Again, it's an educational issue. In Kashgar, only about
7 percent of high school students in the city are from rural
households, though the vast majority of households in
Kashgar—92 percent—are rural. This shows that the matri-
culation rate for Uyghur children in Kashgar is extremely low.
Poverty is an educational issue, and people are indeed desti-
tute. It goes back to what I said before about there being
problems in our own education.

SN: The website once attempted to rescue a young girl named
Nurgül, but in the end it didn't work out, correct?

Ilham: We did actually rescue her, and we requested that the
government provide support, but some cadres sat on their
hands and refused to take care of it. That child was rescued,
in the first place, but in the end she wound up back in the same
circumstances.

SN: Do you often think of these children?

Ilham: I think of them often. When I get involved in that sort of
rescue work, I often think of them. Sometimes we get calls at
night seeking our help, and of course we do whatever needs
doing, including sending money to people.

SN: A lot of volunteers have come in during this period.

Ilham: Among those who volunteer to rescue Uyghur children, many of them were Han, but very few were Uyghur. Our young people lack a certain degree of compassion. We ourselves haven't faced these issues squarely—instead, we've simply relied on the government, which won't solve the problem. We can't save every single child ourselves, but we can call for society to pay more attention to them.

SN: The website was blocked in May. Was it temporary?

Ilham: I don't know. The block had received a lot of attention in both the domestic and foreign media.

SN: Why was it blocked?

Ilham: It was suddenly closed one afternoon. To this day it's still not clear why they did that.

SN: Was it retaliation for some articles that were published?

Ilham: It wasn't that. Now and then the relevant organs demand that we remove certain articles, but we won't remove them as long as I think they haven't broken the law.

SN: What sort of difficulties does Uyghurbiz face?

Ilham: Money. Last year we invited experts to translate forty works by Uyghur authors; making these assignments and so forth all requires a lot of money. This year we bought our own server, and we have someone dedicated to maintaining the site. We registered a company, we have our own office, and we opened a Uyghur-language version. Even if we do nothing, just the office itself costs 100,000 yuan (about $16,000). This year we didn't have too many original articles. We had planned to start English- and Turkish-language versions, but now we're having trouble just making ends meet.

SN: Can you run ads?

Ilham: We haven't done any advertisements at all. We're using the word "Uyghur," and I don't want to sell out this word for money. And of course, no one dares to run ads with us either.

SN: There are some vicious attacks against you online. In particular, some say that you harbor splittist intentions. Does this sort of thing prey on your mind?

Ilham: Of course not. Doing what I'm doing, I had to psychologically prepare for it and not be afraid of people attacking me. There is plenty of slander and rumor-mongering on the Uyghurbiz forums, and I never deleted those negative posts. As I said earlier, I am a Chinese patriot and also a humanitarian. We're part of the country, and we absolutely have no intention of splitting it. At the same time, we should also be able to enjoy the protection of the law, and the government should extend this protection.

Returning to Xinjiang after Retirement

SN: Aside from your day job, you run a business as well as a website. Given that you've taken on so many roles, are you still able to focus a lot of energy on teaching?

Ilham: I really like to teach—I love the teaching profession. Last year, Yale University invited me to a conference with scholars from around the world; a few days ago I received another of their invitations, but I didn't go. If it wasn't for teaching, I would have long ago left China, like many of my colleagues.

SN: Will you stay in Beijing after you retire?

Ilham: I won't. I'm going to go back to Xinjiang. I wanted to go back years ago, but the environment in Xinjiang is bad in so many different ways that I just can't do anything there. I just think that there are so many opportunities for study and work in Beijing, but apart from that I don't have too much attachment to the place.

SN: Do you think you'll be able to integrate into Xinjiang society when you return?

Ilham: There's not a question of being able to integrate or not. In the first place, I travel back and forth to Xinjiang from Beijing several times a year. I'm also in contact with Uyghurs in Beijing on a regular basis, and I study Uyghur social issues. I love the people of my homeland. I love the land I was raised on, and my heart belongs to it even though I live in the interior.

SN: Do you ever get tired, thinking of so many issues, traveling so much?

Ilham: I don't feel it; maybe I get a bit tired. But I won't slack off. If I have nothing on, then I just read books or read things online. I don't look after myself very well. Sometimes I don't eat from morning to night, and I don't even realize.

SN: If you can't relax, does that mean you're not able to put a lot of your time and energy into your children and family?

Ilham: That's true. From yesterday to today, I haven't seen my daughter.

SN: Does she get mad at you?

Ilham: She doesn't. But I know she gets a bit upset. That in turn upsets me, her father.

We Uyghurs Have No Say

This interview was published by iSunAffairs¹ on December 13, 2012. The interviewer is Zhao Sile.

iSunAffairs: What's your view of the recent "Xinjiang Nut Cake" incident?²

Ilham Tohti: There's something strange about the way the police handled it. They haven't been very clear or rigorous about the information they've released. For example, was the level of compensation set by the police or by the Uyghur vendor? From Weibo, it seems that some people were also injured in this incident, but the police haven't given a clear explanation on this point.

I don't believe that the "Two Fewer, One Leniently" policy³ has had much of an effect. When Uyghurs are evicted from their homes as part of urban redevelopment projects, they don't necessarily end up with 160,000 yuan. Recently, I've come across cases of Uyghurs who have come to Beijing to petition because they didn't receive reasonable compensation

---

1 *iSunAffairs* was a current affairs weekly founded in Hong Kong in 2011. In May 2013 it closed down shortly after its publisher was attacked on the street. The attackers were never identified.—Editors

2 Xinjiang nut cake is a Uyghur food made of nuts and dried fruits. In December 2012, a Han villager in Yueyang, Hunan Province, got into a fight with a Uyghur vendor over the price of the cake. It quickly escalated into a group fight between Han villagers and Uyghur vendors in the area. The incident subsequently became national news.—Editors

3 The "Two Fewer, One Leniently" Policy: According to a 1984 policy document issued by the CPC Central Committee, "We must stick to a policy of 'Arresting Fewer and Executing Fewer' ethnic minority criminals and generally handle their cases leniently."

when their houses were torn down. For example, several dozen households only received 350 yuan per square meter when they were evicted in Shamalbagh, Kashgar.

Did the police give 160,000 yuan in compensation because that Uyghur was the stronger party? I can't accept that the way the police acted in this incident reflected their ordinary attitude; I think there were political factors at work.

Getting rid of the "Two Fewer, One Leniently" policy is easy. The policy has actually never been implemented in ethnic regions, so it doesn't really exist there. Getting rid of the policy would be a political "bonus point" by showing responsiveness to the public.

Actually, a lot of Uyghurs have left other parts of China as the environment for them has worsened, particularly with the increase in ethnic tensions since the July 5th Incident. Very few Uyghurs are still engaged in petty trade throughout China, far fewer than before 2009. Meanwhile, we've found that there's been a serious expansion in online troublemaking over petty theft by Uyghur teenagers, especially after Zhang Chunxian came out and announced a policy of "bringing Xinjiang's street children home." After so many years, more than 1,600 of them. As these problems spread, political factors play a role to some degree.

iSunAffairs: What do you think the collective ridicule directed toward this incident says about the attitude of the Han public?

Ilham Tohti: Of course, I don't want to defend the pushy selling of Xinjiang nut cake or other unlawful behavior. I have the same views on this type of behavior as many other people: it's unlawful and unethical and should be handled according to laws and policies. I oppose the "Two Fewer, One Leniently" policy and think that ethnic groups shouldn't get any special treatment on this point. I also won't deny that a lot of Uyghurs are engaged in bad behaviors throughout China, such as selling drugs, theft, and fraud. Those people are taking advantage of Uyghurs and Han alike. But the rate of crime and vagrancy among Han in Xinjiang is also quite high. Different ethnic groups aren't very different on these scores.

But what I can't stand is when the acts of individuals are used to condemn all Uyghurs as a group. Should we condemn all Han for the actions of Wang Zhen? [Note: Wang Zhen was a People's Liberation Army general who governed Xinjiang for a long time after 1949 and brutally repressed local ethnic groups there.] Should we blame all Han because of the poisoned milk powder scandal?

People in Xinjiang are suffering from many of the same things that Han suffer from in the rest of China, like forced evictions and land appropriation. And those with power in Xinjiang are almost entirely Han. It would be unfair to start labeling and condemning "you people" because of acts committed by a few individuals, an institution, a company, or a group. Every day in Xinjiang there are Han who steal and murder. Should we then talk about them as "Han murderers"? This kind of labeling isn't right. Let individuals take responsibility for their own acts.

The fact that Han people have paid such attention to this incident online shows their attitude toward Uyghurs. That's the real issue. Some Han people have gone on an online crusade against Uyghurs as a people. That kind of attitude is extremely dangerous. Han people have a certain degree of freedom of expression, but Uyghurs don't. That's a serious problem. For example, many people are attacking Uyghurs online, and there's a great deal of ethnic discrimination. No matter whether you look at it from an academic perspective, from a human rights perspective, or from the view of the West, it's ethnic discrimination. Han people need to reflect more on their own nationalist and fascist attitudes.

Over the past twenty years, Han people—especially the younger generation—have grown up drinking the wolf's milk of nationalism. They are very emotional and angry, and their chauvinism is quite serious. To put it bluntly, some in Han society have turned fascist against us. There are already "skin-heads" targeting Uyghurs. This kind of thinking, these emotions—it's very dangerous.

The reality is that China is ruled by the Han. So they should bear some responsibility for this country and for our fate. You're the ones who have made us integrate. You're leading us, and as leaders you must take responsibility and be inclusive and tolerant. If 1.3 billion Han cannot tolerate 10 million Uyghurs, then how can you talk about unity or harmony?

iSunAffairs: What accounts for this phenomenon, in your view?

Ilham Tohti: For one thing, since 1989 the authorities have encouraged nationalism as a check against Western influence. Domestically, they've highlighted the problems in Tibet and Xinjiang. They find excuses to reinforce their rule and main-tain stability. They use their strict policies of control and their ethnic policies in Tibet and Xinjiang to cover up a lot. On the other hand, nobody wants to take responsibility for reform. Just as in the rest of China, the organs of stability have turned into an interest group. In Xinjiang it's an even bigger problem than in most other provinces and municipalities. There are the more than 2.6 million people in the Xinjiang Production and Construction Corps, plus huge deployments of soldiers, armed police, and border guards. There are also a lot of government agencies devoted to preserving stability. There are quite a few central government bodies focused on stability in Tibet and Xinjiang, too. It's become a huge interest group—they need there to be problems to survive. And they have power.

If Xinjiang didn't have any problems, who would let these guys in the Politburo? Would they get allocated so much per-sonnel, so much money, so many projects?

iSunAffairs: Have the voices of Uyghur intellectuals been included in government policy-making regarding Xinjiang?

Ilham Tohti: At the central level, Xinjiang policy is set by the Central Politics and Law Commission, where there's a Central Coordinating Office on Xinjiang Work. The head of that office is Zhou Yongkang, and the number two is Wang Lequan. There are no Uyghurs in that office.

The State Council on Ethnic Affairs has a Center on Ethnic Research, which acts as a think tank for central government policy-makers. There's not a single Uyghur there, either. After the July 5th Incident, a lot of research teams were sent to Xinjiang and there were numerous conferences held in Beijing. I'm not aware of a single Uyghur being invited to take part.

iSunAffairs: Are you under pressure for continuing to speak out about Xinjiang?

Ilham Tohti: I face pressure and misunderstanding all the time. The government once said it wanted to hear my views and invited me to write some articles for the central government. I took up the offer and handed in one report after another, a whole bunch of recommendations. But I've become too disillusioned, and I don't write anymore.

The first time I was approached by the state security authorities was in 1994. That was after I published a couple of research reports in Chinese journals, "Analysis of the Educational and Economic Factors Influencing the Quality of the Uyghur Population" and "The Problem of Uyghur Excess Labor." In those reports, I questioned the veracity of a lot of government data. It was on account of those reports that the state security authorities came to get me in Xinjiang and my nightmare began. My mother just about went crazy!

It was my advisor who saved me at the time. He had recommended my research to the higher-ups at my school and I had received some prizes. Later, I also received awards in Beijing. After that, state security didn't bother me again about those things. Otherwise, I'd very likely be in prison right now. After that, they wouldn't let me take part in national-level research projects or university research projects. All of my courses were gradually canceled and I wasn't allowed to teach.

For the past six months, my internet access at home and on my phone has been basically cut off. The slightest thing, like some meeting or a visit by a state leader—even things I never heard about—will lead to my internet getting cut. I still get charged by my internet provider and the phone company, but I can't get online. Sometimes the police will keep watch over my home or summon me for endless "interviews."

I've actually found a way to communicate with those "higher-ups." When the security police come to harass me, I tell them everything I want to make sure gets heard. That's my only platform now. I think that as long as I continue to speak the truth, sooner or later it will have some effect.

iSunAffairs: What impact does the loss of Uyghur intellectuals' voices have?

Ilham Tohti: The role of Uyghur intellectuals as a secular, neutral force in Uyghur society has been shrinking. After the July 5th Incident, quite a few intellectuals, online personalities, and media figures have been sent to prison.

With its secular forces under pressure, Uyghur society is becoming increasingly closed-off and isolated. As a result, it's the more negative and closed-minded forces that are driving Uyghur society now. We once had our own perfectly good system of clothing, culinary culture, and music. Why are these now all becoming increasingly Islamicized? It's because ordinary people have lost all hope in their government, in society, in Uyghur intellectuals, and in secularism. The government was first to destroy the forces of secularism. These should have been most able to interact with Han society and the government, but the government destroyed them instead. So Uyghur society has moved in a completely different direction and become distorted.

iSunAffairs: What are the main ways that inequality between Han and Uyghurs manifests itself?

Ilham Tohti: Power. Do you really believe that Han run all the businesses in Xinjiang because they're so much more capable? No—today's China is not a market economy: capitalism here is all access to power.

Xinjiang is even more so. Power is the core problem—everything else can be dealt with through gradual adjustments. Actually, it's easy to understand why there are some inequalities between ethnic groups. But we cannot accept inequality that is the result of power.

The authorities take advantage of ethnic conflicts in order to solidify their control over power. And the more control they have, the more that power comes into conflict with the interests of Uyghurs.

To a certain degree, both Han and Uyghurs are being controlled in Xinjiang. It's very tragic that many Han suffer persecution and then go on to support this current type of regime anyway.

iSunAffairs: Do you think democratization of China's political system would help to resolve the Xinjiang issue?

Ilham Tohti: I don't think it would resolve the Xinjiang problem once and for all. It might not even help to ameliorate the problem, either, since there could be violence after democratization. I don't see a lot of good prospects for Xinjiang. Just look at the bad feelings on both sides, with extremist feelings among Uyghurs and "Great Han Chauvinism" among the Han. And extremist anti-Uyghur views among the Han have gotten more serious since July 5 than anti-Han extremism among Uyghurs.

Xinjiang's economy will definitely weaken after democratization, because all of the enterprises and projects that the Han have spread throughout Xinjiang through their planned economy will leave once China democratizes. But the political structure will change in all parts of Xinjiang. Setting aside the capacity for political mobilization and just looking at the population structure, even without ethnic autonomy the status of Uyghurs would rise with democratization, including influence and language and culture.

But unless Uyghur intellectuals get support from the government and have the right to speak up and increase their influence in Xinjiang before this process of democratization begins, there will be fighting and bloodshed. Enhanced communication between Uyghur and Han elites and promotion of social interactions might prevent the specter of long-term conflict.

iSunAffairs: Do you feel that Han intellectuals show enough understanding and support for the situation facing Uyghurs?

Ilham Tohti: I've always made a point of having contacts with Han intellectuals. But I feel that in their research and reports—including a lot of what the media reports, too—a lot of them aren't interested in finding a win-win situation for both Han and Uyghurs. Instead, they're most concerned about how the government ought to control and manage us. This is where the problem lies. Uyghur intellectuals aren't going to help you control and manage the Uyghur people. There's no way for us to reach consensus on this, because what you're doing is wrong, it's political.

I eventually grew tired of discussing this issue with my Han friends.

But things are now following a negative trend, where the responsibility is being shifted toward Uyghurs and particularly Uyghur intellectuals. They say we should proactively make changes and take back our criminals and street children.

What a joke! Do we have that kind of say in the matter? If you were to try that and organize even twenty people, the *guobao* would immediately come and take you away. We're a people with no say over our own society, our own education, even our own language!

Why the Uyghurs Feel Defeated

This 2013 interview was conducted by Radio France Internationale (RFI) on the fourth anniversary of the July 5th Incident in Urumqi.

New Structural Changes in Uyghur Society

RFI: Beginning in April [2013] with the violent incident in Maralbexi County, there have been another two violent attacks within the last three days. It appears that these incidents are becoming more frequent. How do you understand this?

Ilham Tohti: I'm not a modern-day Zhuge Liang [military strategist during the Three Kingdoms period], but in fact in 2009 when I was detained, I discussed this with the authorities. At the time, I made the bold prediction that the instances of violent conflict in Xinjiang would increase over the next five or ten years, and that isolated incidents might coalesce into a movement. The presupposition for my comment at the time was that the authorities should use the opportunity to fix their Xinjiang policies and show the public that they can express their demands rationally, peacefully, and through the law— and that this will result in solutions to problems.

But, looking at things as they stand now, the authorities didn't get it done. Now, people don't believe that they can solve any problems through reasoned, peaceful, lawful means. Also, the situation recently has changed a lot, particularly in the rural areas. Over these years, China's entire labor market has changed and prices have been constantly on the rise. Now, there is a huge shortage of Han migrant workers; in Xinjiang

in the 1950s, 1960s, and even until the 1980s, farmers, elementary school students, middle-school students, high-school
students, and technical school graduates could all find jobs in
enterprises. But now, Han and private companies have stopped
recruiting, as well as state companies. Farmers in rural areas
don't have much arable land, and increased urbanization and
industrialization has also exacerbated the competition for
resources between urban and rural. Forced demolitions and
the establishment of economic development zones has also led
to Uyghur farmers possessing less arable land.

Further, the young people here are in a very similar situation to young people elsewhere in China—they're not
interested in inefficient, low-income labor; they're not willing
to travel to backwards areas and engage in farm labor, because
that sort of work simply doesn't satisfy their spiritual and
material demands.

Meanwhile, Uyghur farmers differ from Han farmers,
because the Han can simply move to cities or transfer to the
service industry, or become workers. The way out for Uyghurs,
on the other hand, is extremely narrow—it's either serving in
a Uyghur restaurant or working at one of the few Uyghur
enterprises. And now many of the Uyghur university graduates are unemployed and find themselves competing with
farmers for jobs. This means that Uyghur graduates are being
turned into factory workers and farmers, while the plight of
Uyghur farmers becomes more and more miserable. Chinese
scholars, however—whether official scholars or not—have
simply not picked up on this trend. That is to say, they have
not grasped the changes in the social fabric of Uyghur society.
They just look at GDP, not the problems behind GDP.

RFI: Given that the entire labor market is as you say, the Han
are also seeing a labor shortage, but they still have the
opportunity to move to cities; meanwhile, Uyghur farmers
face a severe problem getting work, with even university
graduates losing employment in large numbers. Does this have

anything to do with the mass migration into Xinjiang from the Chinese interior?

Ilham Tohti: It's not only that. Another problem is that over the last four to five years, Xinjiang has been all about these massive housing projects for low-income people. But upon looking at the data, it turns out that many of the apartments were assigned to the army corps and new migrants. Scholars at the Chinese Academy of Social Sciences told me that someone did a study in Aksu prefecture and found that the low-income or affordable housing units were not actually inhabited by locals. Meanwhile, Xinjiang has been constructing a large number of economic development zones, which has led to industrial pollution being transferred to Xinjiang, along with huge capital, migrants—and inflation. In 2009, 30 yuan bought a kilo of lamb, but now the cost is 60 yuan. Can regular people still afford to eat meat? Xinjiang authorities have been talking up how much they've improved the people's livelihood over these years, but what I see is that it's precisely over the last four or five years that the common people in Xinjiang—in particular Uyghurs—have seen the most severe deterioration in their standard of living.

The Authorities Should Help Minorities Succeed, Not Make Them Fail

RFI: Apart from standard of living issues, do Uyghurs ever feel that they're discriminated against? And are they, in fact?

Ilham Tohti: I'm not sure if you read Uyghurbiz, but over the last few years we have been paying a lot of attention to equality issues in Xinjiang. This includes issues of discrimination and anti-discrimination. I joked that 2014 was Uyghurbiz's anti-discrimination year, while 2013 was the year when Uyghurs opposed religious discrimination. Prior to 2009, although there were some parts of Xinjiang in which Uyghurs were forbidden from growing out their beards—it wasn't as frenzied and widespread as it later became. This sort of policy is really stupid. Historically, this phenomenon has rarely been seen. Banning beards and restricting what people can wear—bringing such personal things into the realm of the forbidden—didn't even happen during the Cultural Revolution. The authorities break the law by doing this. There is no legal basis for it, and it's the behavior of an underworld mob. When the law is flaunted like that, what are common people supposed to trust and rely on in terms of the government? The result is the Uyghurs are more and more self-enclosed. They're also much more worried. Many Uyghurs are suffering anxiety, and many are asking: what are we supposed to do? What is this way of treating Uyghur people in Xinjiang? They should be helping this people succeed! They should be helping to achieve their political, social, economic, and cultural success. But in Xinjiang the authorities are doing the opposite, using methods of control that lead to Uyghur failure. Trying to use this means to unite and stabilize Xinjiang is fruitless. It will simply lead to ethnic opposition.

RFI: Do you mean that only by helping them succeed will it be possible for Uyghurs to live and work in peace, and make them feel as though they're part of the larger national family?

Ilham Tohti: Yes. But now they have a feeling of having been thwarted, a sense of failure. This isn't merely a rural problem— it goes for intellectuals, cadres, students; it's across social strata. In the past I was always optimistic about Xinjiang, but now I'm very worried. I can give my own circumstances as an example; if I were Han, would I be in my current predicament? For so many years, I have always simply been an advocate of dialogue, wanting to give constructive suggestions, to alleviate social tensions, and to bridge the dissonance and the gap between Uyghurs and the government and Uyghurs and Han people. And yet this has made me a target of suppression—a suppression that has become more and more ferocious. So think about it, with this approach, how is Xinjiang going to end up?

Suppression as a Collective Sentiment

RFI: Why don't they seek to mediate? Do the authorities suppress because they're scared? If so, what exactly are they afraid of?

Ilham Tohti: One reason is that the authorities know that the problems in Xinjiang are numerous, and that they haven't done the right thing. They also know the feelings of the public, so they're scared. There have been some changes in the regions west of Xinjiang, including in the Middle East and Central Asia, including changes in ideology and political movements. The authorities may be concerned that these changes will impact Xinjiang. Another aspect is that Xinjiang itself harbors all manner of possibilities—it's a concentration of so many of China's social contradictions. Whatever contradictions exist elsewhere in China, also exist in Xinjiang; and Xinjiang has problems that other places don't, some of which are even more salient.

RFI: Amid the regime's anxiety, it seems that what they fear most is Xinjiang becoming independent. Do you think that there is a strong separatist force?

Ilham Tohti: It seems on the surface that what the authorities fear most is separatism, but my view is that they're perfectly clear about their ability to deal with that. The fact is that separatism is just not a strong force in Xinjiang, and there is no real organization advocating it. Perhaps what the authorities fear instead is the Uyghur people having their own ethnic and cultural identity. This is a collective identity of a people, and when the suppression becomes a collective sentiment, of course the authorities get scared. Why don't they fear the Han common folk? Because they don't have a feeling of collective suffering. Each individual feels that things are unequal or unreasonable, but they don't share that sense collectively. But Uyghurs, due to their common belief, have a sense of themselves as a people, and this collective identity is growing stronger. When religious activities are suppressed—or, for instance, when I'm put under house arrest, maybe other Uyghurs see that and think: we're all being put under house arrest. When you're not allowed to go to the mosque and pray, everyone will feel the sense that they're being repressed. This is a collective feeling, the feeling of a people. What the authorities in Xinjiang fear is that the Uyghurs will develop their own sense of themselves as a people, their religious identity, and a sense of their history.

The Government Should Uphold What Is Right

RFI: If I haven't misunderstood, [you're saying that] there are two causes for the increased frequency of violent outbursts in Xinjiang: the first is economic pressure and unequal treatment in employment and so on, and the other is that the authorities have not tried to help this people succeed, or supported them. Does this have to do with the direction that official policies have taken?

Ilham Tohti: The authorities are simply using their familiar tools on Xinjiang: high-pressure tactics. Look what has been increasing the most over the last few years in Xinjiang: police, armed police, auxiliary police, and other "stability maintenance" forces. We've reviewed a number of court judgments, and they are increasingly frequent and the means of punishment increasingly severe. In February people were sent to jail for using the internet. I believe there were twenty people sentenced; the crime was that they had saved some articles from foreign websites onto USB drives. According to Xinhua, they were sent to prison for six years. More recently, nineteen people were sentenced for the crime of going on foreign websites and watching foreign videos. They were sentenced for five years.

Can ordinary people live under these conditions? As a university professor in Beijing, I also feel that the plight of Uyghurs is becoming more and more severe. The authorities should know that whatever policy they pursue in Xinjiang, it needs to be just, fair, and have people feel that no matter your ethnicity you're going to receive equal treatment. The government must treat people with equality and uphold justice. There will always be discrimination between groups—it exists in France and in America. But the nation and the government itself must stand for what is right. The basis for this is the law, morality, and local history. But the authorities have precisely neglected all these questions in Xinjiang— they've simply considered a few short-term policies, then concealed or misrepresented what they're really about.

Uyghurs Are Increasingly Less Represented in Power

RFI: I'm under the impression that the government says that it has been investing large sums of capital into Xinjiang over the years, that it wants unity among the peoples, and that it has done things that are beneficial to everyone.

Ilham Tohti: What you just said is indeed what they're saying in China. But the key thing is that what the authorities have done has not actually brought any concrete changes. What does the kind of investment the authorities have arranged, so-called "helping Xinjiang policies," have to do with the Uyghur people? The distribution [of influence and resources] between groups is increasingly unfair. Just looking at political power, from the central to the local government, there are fewer and fewer Uyghurs represented. There are fifteen Standing Committee members in the Xinjiang Uyghur Autonomous Region, and just four are Uyghurs. At the central government level, it used to be that there were always two, one People's Political Consultative Conference vice-chair and one National People's Congress Standing Committee vice-chair. Now there is only one NPC vice-chair, and this vice-chair is also often the chair of the Xinjiang People's Congress Standing Committee. But this person is not a member, or even an alternate member, of the Central Committee, nor are they a member of the Party committee that rules the XUAR.

RFI: How do Uyghur cadres fare at the grassroots level—are they the majority in Xinjiang?

Ilham Tohti: It used to be that a Uyghur was the vice-secretary of Xinjiang, but that's no longer the case. In every region, from the Public Security Bureau to the Political and Legal Affairs Commission, there are some places where the Uyghur posts are empty. In some places those spots have been occupied by smaller minorities. What's different now, however, is that the Xinjiang government is more clever, and they know their propaganda. They do propaganda better than they used to. It seems that they've paid a lot of attention to this, so the propaganda makes it seem that the authorities are very concerned with Uyghur livelihood and rights. But what we've actually seen is that whatever the authorities have done in Xinjiang, it hasn't been about improving the rights of Uyghurs, nor has it been about the inequalities in Xinjiang society, including the inequality between ethnic groups. Further, in the last few years this inequality has become more and more acute. Uyghurs feel increasing unease.

Now Is a Key Moment in the Adjustment of Xinjiang Policy

RFI: You sound more pessimistic than in our last interview. How do you think the Xinjiang issue is going to be resolved, in the end?

Ilham Tohti: At the moment I'm not as pessimistic as many others—though I'm not particularly optimistic either. In 2009, and 2010 when Zhang Chunxian became Party Secretary of Xinjiang, I felt that we might have been witnessing the dawn of a new era, and that we'd see some adjustments [in Xinjiang policy]. The Xinjiang authorities have now lost the best opportunity. Although I also believe that as long as Party Central, the Xinjiang Party Committee, and Secretary Zhang

Chunxian are all deeply committed, there is still definitely enough time—it's not that the horse has already left the barn, as some say. What I'm pessimistic about is simply that I had high hopes over the last few years, but the Xinjiang authorities truly have let the best opportunity they had slip by. Yet—there's still a chance. Xinjiang has so many problems. Can we urgently turn things around, commit to resolving them with speed and wisdom, and make a big adjustment? What sort of adjustment? They need to listen to the variety of opinions from the Uyghur people themselves. If the authorities feel that formal channels are politically impractical for that, then perhaps they could use informal methods? For instance, hold forums, organize some official survey teams—not like last time, which had enormous scale but was merely for show.

I think that right now is the key moment for revising policy. Also, the former director of the State Ethnic Affairs Commission, who was of Mongolian extraction, has become a secretary in the Communist Party's Secretariat and a secretary-general in the State Council, so I think this marks the beginning of a major revision in ethnic policy. There's another angle, which is that previously the Central Xinjiang Coordination Office (中央新疆协调办公室) used to be located under the Politico-Legal Commission (政法委), and now it's been moved to the State Ethnic Affairs Commission, and the head of that commission is one of the members. So I believe that this may be the beginning of an adjustment.

Prolonged High Pressure and Resistance May Become Part of the Culture of the Uyghur People

RFI: What exact policy adjustments do you think there will be? Alleviating the repression, livelihood, welfare, equal opportunity, increased inter-ethnic communication?

Ilham Tohti: The new leaders need a period of time after assuming power; we don't have a clear read on what their policies were in other parts of China. I think that now is the best time for adjustments, but some problems have cropped up in Xinjiang. When incidents happen, the authorities simply want to crush, repress, crack down—high pressure on top of pressure—and it creates a vicious spiral. High pressure in Xinjiang simply leads to a heightened backlash. If this continues, resistance will become a culture—it won't be an isolated incident of resistance, or problems in just one village, but the entire people will develop a "resistance culture." I understand my people. They're a people with dreams; they have a strong historical culture and ethnic traditions. If they're not accorded any respect, in this age of openness and the internet, then they might turn to all-out confrontation. It might turn into a whole-people movement.

Maybe my saying this will lead to quite unfavorable consequences, and the authorities will be angry, but I can't not say it: what the authorities are doing is very stupid.

RFI: On the one hand you harbor some hope for the new leadership, and you believe there is still time to solve the problem; on the other hand, you believe they are doing some very stupid things and the policies must be thoroughly changed. If they don't do that, what happens?

Ilham Tohti: Think about it, if they still don't act in time, if they don't change their policies, then what will happen? After China democratizes, what will happen? No one can stop China's transitioning to a democracy. But what I'm most worried about is that the problems created by the government will have to be paid for by both the Han and Uyghur people. If the problem was created by the government and was simply between the government and the people, then it could be resolved by adjustments to government policy, or political change, or goodwill on the part of the government. But if the status quo persists for a long time and morphs into hatred between peoples, then even change in policy or the political system won't be of any use. Only after an entire generation dies off is there hope for that sort of hate to wash out. But this might take a couple of hundred years. China doesn't have that much time. Han people don't have that much time; Uyghurs don't have that much time. So, I hope that right now, whether it's foreign Chinese-language media, scholars inside China, or people in China, that we can all unite and focus on our common problems: people's livelihoods, civil rights, democracy, and the rule of law. We need to support each other, push forward together, and fight for our future together. We call out in hope that a few conflicts won't become bitter conflicts between peoples; and we call for the government to revise its policies and avoid being culpable in the eyes of history.

"The Uyghurs Are Living in Fear"

An interview conducted by Voice of America (VOA) in Beijing in November 2013.

VOA: After the deadly car crash at Tiananmen on October 28 [in which five people died in a fiery crash that the government blamed on the separatist East Turkmenistan Islamic Movement], the only reports available to the Chinese public all have to follow the official reporting from Xinhua. But some overseas media have pointed out that since Tiananmen Square is so densely covered with surveillance cameras, there should be video of the incident from a variety of angles and locations. However, as of today the Chinese official media have not released any video at all. Prof. Ilham Tohti, have you been able to use your Uyghur Online website to publish any independent opinions and report on what actually happened?

Ilham Tohti: On the day of the incident, we issued a statement saying that we shouldn't be in such a hurry to come to a judgment about what happened until there was more evidence. Over the following several days, out of consideration for the safety of others associated with Uyghur Online, I began publishing opinions under my name only. For several days, I was constantly giving media interviews. But there aren't very many of us, and I have to consider other people's safety.

I worry that, in the absence of any nongovernment media outlets, many people will only get their information from official sources. I fear that, just as in the past, this will lead to misunderstanding and hatred. I am hoping that, through VOA and other friends in the media, we will be able to make our own voices heard. We want to stop the ethnic hatred. Uyghurs and Han are friends, not enemies. The primary responsibility for [this incident] rests with the government.

I daresay I can predict what the government's next steps will be, as I've been right about this in the past. In a few days, the government will release video showing several Uyghurs, their faces covered, tearfully apologizing and saying: "I committed wrongdoing!" However, it will be very difficult to confirm the identities of these people and determine whether or not they are actors. Based on the evidence currently being put forward by the government, it's hard for us Uyghurs to believe [that this is a terrorist attack]. If the government actually has evidence of this, it ought to make it public since this would help its case.

"Preferential" Policies toward Uyghurs

VOA: During this year's annual meeting of the National People's Congress, we interviewed some members of the Xinjiang delegation. At that time, the delegates made a point of mentioning all the various kinds of preferential treatment being offered to Uyghurs, like extra points on the university entrance exams, no enforcement of the one-child policy, and bilingual education for ethnic children. What do you think of these preferential policies toward ethnic minorities?

Ilham Tohti: I have long expressed support for bilingual education, but I feel this policy has come too late. What we Uyghurs oppose is being misled with false promises. The so-called bilingual education currently being carried out in Xinjiang is really an education aimed at assimilation into Han culture. The quality of education of Uyghurs is on the decline, and bilingual education is in reality not what it sounds like. Many Uyghur children can't understand Uyghur, and they can't really understand Mandarin Chinese either.

As far as preferential birth-control policies are concerned, it's true that Uyghurs are allowed to have two or three children. But Han Chinese living in Xinjiang are also able to have more than one child. And this is not a policy aimed at Uyghurs; it's aimed at all ethnic minorities in China. On the other hand, I don't really consider this to be a preferential policy. As an ethnic group living in an autonomous region, we ought to be able to establish our own birth-control policies based on our own circumstances. Our population base is relatively small, only 10 million, and 80 percent are poor and live in rural areas that haven't been urbanized or industrialized. The Uyghur population in Xinjiang is also aging, resulting in labor shortages and other problems. Many policies have really hurt us. Currently the male-female sex ratio is severely unbalanced. This is not only a problem for demographers—many people have come to recognize it. Uyghur females outnumber males, and many Uyghur girls are unable to marry.

When it comes to development of the economy, I think the thing Uyghurs feel most upset about is the unfair way that resources are distributed. Extra points on the university exam or preferential birth-control policies are only a small part of the problem, in my opinion. They're not the essential problem. Receiving education in our own language ought to be our right. But over the past decade—especially since 2005—we've been deprived of these rights in Xinjiang. Outsiders don't understand the reality and think we oppose bilingual education. That's not the case. Many Uyghurs were originally illiterate and have begun studying Chinese of their own initiative.

Unfair Distribution of Political Power and Social Resources

VOA: I've heard people make the following argument: Xinjiang is a vast and rich territory, especially with regard to the rich mineral resources underground. If Xinjiang people possessed or controlled those resources, Xinjiang would become China's Kuwait. What rights do you think Uyghurs ought to have over Xinjiang's natural resources?

Ilham Tohti: What I'd say is that the resources we're talking about are not just natural resources. There is also the resource of [political] power. Of the fifteen seats on the Xinjiang Autonomous Region Party Committee, only four go to Uyghurs. Those members are responsible for the labor union, the ethnic and religious affairs committee, and other bodies without any real power. Then there's the regional governor, Nur Bekri, but neither his two assistants nor his driver are Uyghurs. None of the people responsible for departments connected to important matters, like personnel, budget, land, finance, airlines, and railroads, are Uyghurs.

As far as natural resources are concerned, central state-owned companies like PetroChina, Sinopec, and China Nonferrous Mining have monopolized the extraction rights for the resources in Xinjiang. On the other hand, most of the so-called private companies operating in Xinjiang are companies from outside Xinjiang, many of them relying on powerful connections, such as people from their home provinces who serve as officials in Xinjiang.

As for Uyghurs, our problem is survival—more basic than economic development. Some Han scholars contend that Uyghurs and Han face essentially the same problems. To some extent, I agree with them, since we're both facing common problems in terms of human rights, rule of law, and democracy. However, Uyghurs also face a unique problem, one of social resources. We also face other problems like ethnic discrimination and religious issues, with pressures similar to those faced by China's Catholic and Protestant house churches.

But the pressure facing us is even greater than that faced by house churches. This is because of our great differences from mainstream Han culture, including in terms of language, appearance, and religious beliefs. I tell Uyghurs that we're facing two Chinas. The misunderstandings between us and the Chinese public can only be resolved through strengthening mutual interaction and understanding. But when it comes to the government, we all have to work together to promote reform and democratization and fight for our human rights.

Restrictions on Religious Activities

VOA: Can you share with us what you've observed about how Xinjiang Uyghurs exercise freedom of religion and take part in religious activities?

Ilham Tohti: Last March, I wrote two pieces on the subject of religious freedom that were presented at an international academic conference held at the Chinese University of Hong Kong and included a great number of examples and photos. Uyghurs' religion puts them in conflict with the materialism of the Communist Party, so the repression we've faced is actually not a recent phenomenon.

Uyghurs—like Han Chinese—were given an atheist education from an early age. However, we are a religious people. The government has never before tried to control religion in Xinjiang as tightly as it does right now. There are many regulations in Xinjiang, such as prohibiting cadres, state enterprise employees, students, teachers, women, university students, and any children under the age of eighteen from entering mosques. Now I ask you: who *is* allowed to enter mosques?

In Xinjiang, Arabic has become a special language that no one is allowed to teach. If you study Arabic, you might be breaking the law. I want to ask the government, what *isn't* illegal? Where can Uyghurs go to study their own religion? If members of society aren't allowed to study religion, then the government ought to provide an adequate number of Islamic colleges. I know that in the United States and the UK there are such colleges.

VOA: The Chinese government called the October 28 Incident at Tiananmen Square a terrorist attack. Is this a reflection of the increasingly acute trajectory of social and ethnic tensions in Xinjiang?

Ilham Tohti: I don't agree with those who say that ethnic conflict is growing more and more acute. I believe that what's getting more intense is the conflict between Uyghurs and the government. No matter how you want to label it, the choice of Tiananmen for self-immolation, violent resistance, or protest is clearly an expression of dissatisfaction with the government.

Uyghur Online (UyghurBiz)

VOA: Next we'd like to discuss the website you've set up, Uyghur Online. Has this website been blocked in China, or can ordinary netizens in China access it?

Ilham Tohti: Our site has been blocked inside China since July 6, 2009. Now we've moved our servers to the United States. Many people are using iPhones to visit. Before it was blocked, Uyghur Online would get 1.2 to 1.5 million visitors a day. Now we're down to around 300,000 visitors a day. Recently, we also set up a Facebook page and a Twitter account. I think that China's Great Firewall is a failure, because netizens seeking information—Uyghurs included—all know how to get around it.

Han Chinese have other choices. There are plenty of television programs or newspapers that discuss Han culture, history, language, and literature. But there is virtually nothing like this for us. Uyghurs like Uyghur Online because it is the only website that speaks in our own voices. And [by trying to shut it down] the government is now helping to promote Uyghur Online. CCTV called us out by name in 2009, giving us free "advertising." Uyghurs are like that: the more they say they don't like something, the more we'll like it. Articles on Uyghur Online circulate quickly among Uyghurs. I've even heard of illiterate old women who know about things we've published.

Problematic "Visits" to Uyghur Homes and Sources of Uyghur Resentment

VOA: Recently we've seen reports of a phenomenon in Xinjiang known as "visiting." Can you tell us a bit about these "visits"? Who is paying visits to Uyghur homes? Are they village cadres? Do they get permission before making these visits to Uyghur homes?

Ilham Tohti: Uyghur Online has published many pieces on this subject. Many of the conflicts in Xinjiang have their origins in these "visits." Sometimes the "visits" are about your beard, your veil, the religious books or symbols in your home or the carpets Uyghurs use during worship. These "visits" are like the fuse that has set off many conflicts, even involving some Uyghur women.

The Quran is sacred to Uyghurs. Although I currently don't go to mosque every week, I am still a Muslim. Even if I only go to mosque for major holidays a few times a year, whenever someone burns or desecrates the Quran I will definitely be upset. It's because this is our religion, part of what makes us Uyghur. Even materialists who don't believe in Islam get upset about the desecration of religion, as long as they are people of conscience.

Ever since Zhang Chunxian came to Xinjiang as party secretary, the policy has been "one police station per village, one police officer per household." Some of the "visitors" are cadres, but the government also hires or provides subsidies to unemployed people and even juvenile delinquents to do the job. Sometimes regular and tactical police officers are also used. I'd be upset, too, if one of these people charged into my home without permission. Even if it were a university dormitory, as opposed to a private home, I'd still find it unacceptable to have someone barging in like that.

The unhappiness felt by Uyghurs in Xinjiang has many sides to it. There's dissatisfaction about the treatment of our religion, language, and culture, as well as about government policies on things including urban redevelopment, employment, cadre recruitment, passports, and even interference with the clothing we wear.

Uyghurs are systematically excluded and discriminated against in Xinjiang, and the government is leading this. These days, I feel that Uyghurs are undivided internally with respect to their unhappiness toward the government—those feelings are unanimously held.

For all the years the government has been in Xinjiang, it has never cultivated a group of Uyghurs with vested interests in the existing system. A handful have vested interests, but they are few in number and don't represent a significant segment of the Uyghur population. Elsewhere, you see ruling elites try to develop their own interest groups, but in Xinjiang they haven't done this. On this point, I think this shows that Xinjiang policy has been a failure—even this hasn't been accomplished!

VOA: Just now, you mentioned urban redevelopment in Xinjiang. We've seen news about the demolition and renovation of the Old City in Kashgar. Does Xinjiang have the same problems with forced eviction and violent demolitions that exist in the rest of China?

Ilham Tohti: On my most recent trip to Xinjiang, some people from Aqsu came to see me. They said that there was a village there that had been turned into a new urban district where apartments were selling for 4000–5000 yuan per square meter. They seized orchards and some cotton fields, paying the local people 420,000 yuan per hectare and then selling the land to developers for 12 million yuan per hectare. They did this to hundreds, even thousands of hectares of land. Of course the local people weren't happy about this.

There are many conflicts like this in Xinjiang, but it's different there than it is in the rest of China. Elsewhere in China, the media can get involved and there are bloggers and microblogs who can reveal details of this kind of thing. At our university, we had a student from Xinjiang who exposed a case like this, only to have state security police drive more than 400 km to arrest him at his home when he returned to Xinjiang. They immediately put him in handcuffs and shaved his head. Fortunately, I heard about the news that day and called up the officer in charge of my case at the Beijing domestic security unit to ask him to help me complain to his superiors, otherwise I was going to go public. Later, I guess the local police in Xinjiang got word and had the student call me on the telephone to say that he had already returned home.

Barred from Traveling Overseas or Visiting Xinjiang Freely; Guilt toward Family but the Need to Forge Ahead

VOA: On February 2, you were on your way to Indiana University to be a visiting scholar when you were stopped at the airport. What happened?

Ilham Tohti: Actually, this isn't the first time I've been prevented from going overseas. For many years now I've been getting invitations from different universities. However, [the domestic security police] always blocked my travel in advance. Before, when I got an invitation from an American university, they put me under house arrest. This time I was very public, telling everyone that I was going to Indiana. Friends even sent me off and held a little going-away party. In the end, they were very barbaric in the way they prevented me from leaving, refusing me water and forbidding me from using the toilet for over ten hours.

My daughter's in the United States now, but this wasn't her choice. Her original plan was to visit for twenty days and then come back. Later, we figured that she has freedom in America and we couldn't choose for her to lose that freedom again. So, no matter how difficult, it's best for her to stay there.

In addition to keeping me from traveling abroad, they also prevent me from leaving Beijing. Before, in 2009 and 2010, they wouldn't let me travel to Xinjiang. They let me go to Xinjiang in 2011, but only in the company of four security officers. In 2012, I went to Xinjiang accompanied by three security officers. They bought their own plane tickets and accompanied me twenty-four hours a day. They arranged for drivers in Xinjiang and accompanied me wherever I went.

But the domestic security police in Xinjiang don't even listen to their counterparts in Beijing. During the annual NPC meeting in 2012, the Beijing police wanted me to stay in Xinjiang and I agreed. They told me not to write any articles, and I agreed. But when I got to Xinjiang, the security police there didn't want me to stay.

This turned into a real conflict. The domestic security police in Xinjiang are only concerned about Uyghurs in Xinjiang, not the capital. Meanwhile, the domestic security police in Beijing don't concern themselves with Xinjiang Uyghurs. [The Xinjiang security police] publicly said, "We don't want to make trouble for you or for ourselves, so why don't you go back home." My brother, sister-in-law, nieces, nephews, and mother would come to me in tears, asking me to leave. I had no choice and went back to Beijing.

The result? Arrangements for my son's schooling were delayed for a year because they waited until after the NPC meeting was over to add my son's name to my household registration. I only managed to resolve the issue this year, so my son had to start school a year later than other kids his age.

So, sometimes I feel that the path I've chosen not only makes my own life difficult, it also affects my innocent children. Sometimes I hold my son and tell him, "I'm sorry, my son." He doesn't understand and asks, "Sorry for what?" I feel truly guilty about my mother and my family. But this is the path I've chosen. Few among more than 10 million Uyghurs dare to express themselves like me. Since I've been doing this for many years, I'll continue to carry on—even if there's risk of death ahead, I guess I must forge ahead.

It's even gotten to the point where I no longer feel that I belong to my own family. I belong to my people, to my friends, to

China—it's a major responsibility I have. I must promote Uyghur-Han communication and prevent conflict and tragedy when political transition occurs in China in the future. I worry that many issues will evolve into major conflicts between Uyghurs and Han, especially during the democratization process.

If we don't start communicating now, and the government doesn't hear our voices and demands and doesn't know what we're thinking, then there will be trouble. The tragedies that have already occurred in Xinjiang will most likely occur again, and other tragedies might occur as well. We might be experiencing what the Basques have gone through. So, I don't just feel responsible to my people. I believe I have a duty to promote understanding between Uyghurs and Han and a duty, along with my Han friends, to push Han and Xinjiang Uyghurs to move forward together. I'm not only saying these things; I'm prepared to pay any price.

Admiration for Democratic Values but No One's "Running Dog"

VOA: Some people on leftist websites accuse independent Chinese intellectuals of being American running dogs and anti-Chinese traitors. How do you respond to these attacks?

Ilham Tohti: Up to this point, despite my difficulties, I have never sought any financial support from any country. I could never become anyone's running dog. I am my own independent person, a Uyghur intellectual who can think for himself. I am first and foremost responsible to my people, my homeland, my nation. I could never become anyone's running dog.

I hold the American system in great esteem. I like American academic freedom and American values, such as the protection of human rights, respect for the minority, religious and press freedom, and democracy. But the thing is, I'm not an American. I don't believe that Uyghur problems can be solved by America. Ultimately, solving Uyghur problems must rely on dialogue between Uyghurs and Han Chinese. I have contacts with American scholars and even the American media. But I'm also in contact with media from many other countries. America was not the first country to invite me to visit. And I've never been to America; I've been to France.

I like to exchange ideas with Chinese intellectuals like Prof. He Weifang, whom I respect a great deal. China's independent intellectuals are a valuable resource for China and the world. The United States needs rational Chinese intellectuals just like China needs the same in the United States. I really hate these ignorant leftists—they're the running dogs. I don't like to disparage others, but if you want to talk about dogs, they're the ones who are dogs.

A Scholar and a Public Ambassador for the Uyghurs

VOA: The problems in Tibet and Xinjiang have their commonalities and differences. Both have ethnic and religious components, but Tibet has its own spiritual leader in the Dalai Lama, whereas Xinjiang has none. Can you be considered the spiritual leader of Xinjiang's Uyghurs?

Ilham Tohti: I'm really worried that people will make me into some sort of spiritual leader. I've been asked similar questions in the past by international organizations, scholars, and diplomats. But in these past several years I've continually guarded against creating this sort of appearance. I am first and foremost a scholar. These days, I'd much rather be promoting Uyghur-Han communication and serving as an activist for Uyghur rights. In China, Uyghurs shouldn't be afraid to speak out on behalf of their own people. Under normal circumstances, we would be able to have our own representatives and groups. But these are not allowed in the current reality, and in fact it's dangerous.

I'm not trying to call on the international community to do anything. What we need is for the Chinese government to take a more responsible attitude and reflect on its Xinjiang policies.

We shouldn't politicize individual cases and turn them into ethnic cases; we should pay attention to evidence. I'm currently willing to serve as a kind of public ambassador for Uyghurs and communicate with Han Chinese, the Han public and media, and the different peoples and nations of the world. This includes the current government. I want to share the results and findings of my research. I don't want to play the part [of a spiritual leader].

Research Areas

VOA: Are you still teaching classes at China Minzu University? What courses do you teach?

Ilham Tohti: This term I was originally scheduled to teach one course for two hours a week. Last term I taught three courses, ten hours per week. I'm not really an economist, but I'm part of the School of Economics and teach courses related to economics. I'm a Xinjiang expert, and my research area is Xinjiang issues. I also do research on Central Asian issues, where my secondary focus is looking at the influence of Central Asian nationalism on Xinjiang, as well as at relations between China and Central Asia. My focus in these past several years has been the issue of Uyghur rights, looking at the issues and difficulties we face in this period of transition and what the future prospects might be.

The course I teach is "Strategic Scientific Development of the Population, Resources, and Environment of Xinjiang." This course was developed in the mid-1990s and was a very popular topic at that time. In China, it's very hard to change the title of a course once it's set. This is an open course for undergraduates, but the university limits the number of students to between twenty and thirty. But quite often two hundred to three hundred students will come to listen to my lectures, even though sometimes the university will only provide a small classroom that cannot seat everyone.

I used to teach courses in development economics and one called "Politics, Society, Economy, and Culture of Central Asia." I ordinarily don't use a textbook, and each time my lectures are different, based on my own preparation and my own research.

In my last class, I played a video discussing the breakup of the Soviet Union and Eastern Europe and the ensuing ethnic conflicts and tragedies. I told students that we must avoid these kinds of problems. Some students asked me for a copy of this video. Things are freer in the classroom. Of course, the government doesn't like this. They videotape me every time I teach, and the government sends people to attend my classes. But it doesn't bother me. They might be listening or taping while I'm teaching, but I don't feel like I'm doing anything secretive and believe I ought to face them openly in the light of day.

VOA: Everything that you've done has actually helped to promote mutual understanding between Han Chinese and Uyghurs. You've also offered some real insights into how the government ought to govern Xinjiang, even if some of your ideas are not entirely in line with the way the government thinks and acts.

Ilham Tohti: I want what's best for everyone—Uyghurs, Han, and the government. But the problem now is that the government is not doing well. If we're doing well, that means the government is doing well. If we're not doing well, it means the government isn't doing well. Right now, things aren't going well for Uyghurs. No matter what the government says, we're still not doing well. When things start to improve for us Uyghurs, that will mean that we have a good government.

Autonomy and Peaceful Co-existence

VOA: After the breakup of the Soviet Union, some of the former Soviet republics where people have religious beliefs similar to yours became new independent Central Asian nations. The Chinese government has made it clear numerous times that it cannot allow Xinjiang to become independent. How do you view this issue?

Ilham Tohti: Over history, Uyghurs have demanded independence. This is normal for an ethnic people. I've studied the global situation and Chinese and Xinjiang history. I've also studied the history of the Basque people and the ethnic problems of the former Soviet Union and Central Asia. I believe that the best option for Uyghurs is to be part of a federal China where democracy and human rights are guaranteed and Uyghurs enjoy self-rule. This would be the best outcome for Han, China, and Uyghurs alike.

A dictatorship without democracy, human rights, or rule of law is no good for any ethnic group and should be considered a tragedy for all. But Uyghurs will not accept a democratic nation where citizens have rights but ethnic groups are granted no power or autonomy.

Spain is a democracy, but democracy has been unable to solve the Basque issue. In Belgium and the UK, we also see different cultural zones. So, many [Chinese] liberal scholars say that everyone will be treated alike as long as China has democracy and civil rights. But this isn't actually true. We have our own unique identity and our own history. What I hope for even more, then, is ethnic autonomy inside China—this is the best possible outcome. If that happened, the Central Asian countries ought to envy us Uyghurs, rather than the other way around.

The Uyghur people possess many strategic resources. If China cherishes this people and puts a good system in place, the Uyghurs could play an important role in China's global strategy with respect to Central Asia and Southwest Asia, rather like the Tatars in Russia. Historically, Uyghurs have gone through periods where they had a high degree of autonomy. This territory once gave birth to the Silk Road. These days, everyone takes their own rights and culture very seriously. The more globalized we become, the more seriously we take our individual cultures, including what makes us unique. The things that differentiate us from others are the things most worth cherishing. Uyghurs take their own rights more and more seriously and focus more and more on their present and future. So we need to talk with each other and resolve the problems between Uyghurs and Han. The solution is not killing, but rather peaceful dialogue. Peaceful coexistence is much better!

An Autonomous Region with No Autonomy

VOA: Records show that when the Chinese Communist Party first took power they had planned to call Xinjiang the "Xinjiang Autonomous Region." At that time, the Uyghur leader Saifuddin told Mao Zedong that autonomy should belong to a people, not to a piece of land. Since the autonomy was for the Uyghurs, the central government listened to his advice and named Xinjiang the "Xinjiang Uyghur Autonomous Region." Has Xinjiang today achieved the kind of autonomy that Uyghurs hope for?

Ilham Tohti: Let's look back at the history. In 1884, the Uyghurs were made an autonomous region of the Qing Empire. Twenty years later, there was no more Qing Empire. At that time, Uyghurs, like Han Chinese, stopped recognizing the Qing. Uyghurs also wanted their national independence and continuously fought for it until 1947.

In 1946, Chiang Kai-shek was smart and sent General Zhang Zhizhong to negotiate a settlement agreement in which he got some Uyghur nationalists from outside China and some Uyghurs then living outside of Xinjiang to form a coalition government. In those days, apart from foreign relations and national defense, everything else was decided in Xinjiang. Xinjiang held its first democratic elections, for local councils, regional councils, and the provincial council. Besides some representatives sent by the government, there were also representatives from the Kazakh people and other ethnic groups.

To tell the truth, that was a truly autonomous Uyghur government, which even retained its own army.

Then, the first constitution under the Communists in 1954
established China as a multiethnic nation and promised ethnic
autonomy. Uyghurs were supportive of this notion of a multiethnic nation. Under the Communists, the laws establishing a
system of autonomy for ethnic regions became one of the fundamental institutions of China. Then the Xinjiang Uyghur
Autonomous Region was established. At that time, there were
many different ideas about how to name this autonomous
region: Turkestan Autonomous Region, Chinese Turkestan
Autonomous Region, Uyghur Autonomous Region, or even
just Turkestan.

Uyghurs especially dislike the name "Xinjiang." I don't like
it either. Before 1884, this region wasn't known as Xinjiang.
Why should the place where Uyghurs live be known by a Han
name as the "New Border Region"? Now, after so many years
of immigration, the population structure of Xinjiang has
changed. Some of the peoples who have lived in Xinjiang "for
generations" really only immigrated there during the Qing or
the Nationalist period. Other than Uyghurs and Tajiks, all the
other ethnic groups are immigrants. A lot of the region's history
has been created to serve official needs. Of course we recognize
our own history. No matter what the percentage of Han in the
population, Uyghur subjectivity and history must be respected.

In 2010, the government published a set of contradictory
data showing that the Han population had increased by nearly
500,000. But the true internal data showed that Han accounted
for 31 percent of the population, whereas the published figures
put it at more than 40 percent. Even though the population
structure has changed somewhat after so many years, Uyghurs
are still the largest ethnic group in Xinjiang. After the Han,
Uyghurs are the second largest cultural group in all of China.
Even though the Zhuang people (壮族) are larger in terms of
population, when it comes to similarities and differences of

language and culture, Uyghurs' fervor for their own culture is growing stronger.

This has encouraged Uyghurs to struggle for their rights, but their demands put them in conflict with government policies. So what should we do? Some think that only independence can solve the problem. Why? It's because many Uyghurs don't understand what autonomy really means. When they discover what the "autonomy" they've been given really means, they say: "We don't want autonomy, we want independence." I think that the problem today is that Xinjiang's "autonomy" is in name only. Real autonomy is something different.

If we had true autonomy and Xinjiang were governed by Uyghurs themselves, then the human rights of each ethnic group would be protected and Uyghurs would have cultural, civic, and economic power. If Uyghurs enjoyed cultural autonomy, we could co-exist peacefully with the Han and we would be able to contribute to China and enjoy the economic development made possible in a large country. This would be a contribution to the country and to the entire world, like the contributions we made during the era of the Silk Road. That's the future I imagine for Xinjiang and the Uyghurs.

Policy Recommendations to the Politburo in 2011

VOA: There have recently been a series of violent incidents in Xinjiang. Following on the April incident in Maralbeshi (Bachu) County and the June incident in Pichan (Shanshan) County, there was another disturbance in July in Hotan. Since the October 28 incident at Tiananmen, security in Xinjiang has suddenly been increased. Some Western media have suggested that the Chinese government ought to reflect on its ethnic policies in Xinjiang and that relying on "strike hard" campaigns and stability maintenance won't bring harmony and unity between Uyghurs and Han in Xinjiang. What recommendations do you have for how to solve Xinjiang's ethnic problems?

Ilham Tohti: Over the past decade, Uyghurs in Xinjiang have been living in a state of relative fear. They don't speak up, out of fear of being arrested. The government has increased the repression and adopted high-pressure policies to achieve stability. I've heard about some of these policies even being in force here in Beijing. Some of the pressure is direct: for example, searches of hotels where Uyghurs stay or preventing landlords from renting to Uyghurs. On WeChat and Weibo I've seen rumors circulating about Uyghurs, for example, that they're using Hami melons to spread disease in the rest of China.

In 2011, I wrote a letter to the Politburo and had it delivered through the security officer who was then in charge of my case. At that time, I pointed out that autonomy didn't mean separatism. I said that if the Chinese Communist Party still believed that it represents the nation, including ethnic minorities, then it ought to take responsibility. I said if it didn't start taking responsibility immediately, then the future would hold it accountable for its crimes.

I discussed the dangerous nature of the situation. Even though we don't take part in legislating now, in the future it will be necessary to find a balance between state law and autonomy before formulating legislation. The right to autonomy needs to be implemented in order to send a sign of goodwill to ethnic minorities. I still continue to stick to this opinion. If the government isn't responsible to the nation and to the future, it will start to lose control over many problems and lose control over the way things are headed.

There are more and more conflicts under this political system—what's the solution? If you don't deal with them, things will become more and more dangerous. Once ethnic conflict erupts and a separatist movement begins, it will definitely lead to tragedy. We've already seen this kind of tragedy in Chechnya. The Chechen independence movement was hard to repress, and people from all different ethnic groups were the ones who got hurt. So the best way forward is a peaceful and civilized way.

Second, I recommended disbanding the Xinjiang Production and Construction Corps (XPCC). The XPCC has turned into an interest group, one that even possesses its own weapons. If the XPCC were ordinary people or a company, this would be illegal. For the XPCC to possess and use weapons is disastrous for Uyghur-Han relations. It creates hatred.

The XPCC should be disbanded and its institutions turned into ordinary institutions. Its farmers should just be farmers, its workers just workers. Its police should be police and its cadres just cadres. Many people misunderstand me—I've never said that anyone should be kicked out of Xinjiang. For many years now, I've been writing pieces recommending that the XPCC be disbanded and setting out the interests at stake. This is for the sake of China's future, of Uyghur-Han relations, and of Xinjiang's future.

Third, I criticized the religious policies being implemented in Xinjiang. Of course, I tried to give them some face. I wrote my letter in as moderate a tone as possible using language that the central authorities would find acceptable, but I still put the problem to them as clearly as possible. I looked at the history and talked about how to give Uyghurs religious freedom. Later, I was told that the central authorities accepted some of my recommendations. At first, it appeared to me as if they had accepted them. But when you looked again later on, the religious policies became more and more barbaric and things turned bad.

I also wrote to them about the language policy and bilingual education, as we discussed earlier. I told them that bilingual education hadn't come too soon, but rather sixty-plus years too late. The problem now is that what they're doing isn't bilingual education. I'm firmly opposed to the language education policy being carried out now, as are other Uyghurs. The government is using mistaken methods to implement a correct policy, and ordinary Uyghurs and Han people are being left to pay for the consequences. I warned that the government risked being condemned throughout the ages for carrying out a policy like this, and I made recommendations about how a language policy should be carried out.

In my letter to the Politburo, I also mentioned methods of preserving stability. Early on, I was told that the central authorities had read my letter and even that they had sent it to the regional government in Xinjiang. For the first few months, they kept asking me about the issues and details I'd raised in my letter. They even seemed to be making recordings of our discussions. Afterward, they intensified their control measures over me and cut my classes.

When I went to Xinjiang, I discovered that the surveillance on me had gotten much heavier. All the people monitoring me had been replaced one by one. Some of my students had even been forced to disappear. The pressure on me has gotten much greater, and all I can do is try to bear it.

If the government were to permit it, I'd definitely like to leave Beijing. I'd like to spend at least half the year in Xinjiang, because that's what I research. I feel as if I've wronged my mother. She was only twenty-three years old when my father died and raised four children on her own. She's sixty-four now, and her illnesses are all caused by me.

The other day I even wrote my will and gave it to my wife, also to another person who is very close to me. I said that if something should happen to me—even if I should die at the hands of the domestic security or state security police—don't think that I've been killed by Han people and let hatred come between our two peoples.